Upside-Down and Blindfolded

Upside-Down and Blindfolded

Daniel J. Pukstas

iUniverse, Inc.
New York   Bloomington

Upside-Down and Blindfolded

iUniverse books may be ordered through booksellers or by contacting:

iUniverse
1663 Liberty Drive
Bloomington, IN 47403
www.iuniverse.com
1-800-Authors (1-800-288-4677)

ISBN: 978-1-4401-2819-6 (pbk)
ISBN: 978-1-4401-3159-2 (ebook)

Printed in the United States of America

iUniverse rev. date: 3/6/2009

CONTENTS

INTRODUCTION

Travel books written by blind people are relatively rare. A second travel book written by a blind person must be rarer still. I hope this rarity stimulates some curiosity among a good many readers in much the same way that a two-headed calf might. Curiosity has always worked well for the newspapers sold at grocery checkouts; I hope it works the same for me. However, this really isn't a travel book in the traditional sense. Although the book certainly makes mentions of specific places, it doesn't do so with any sense of recommending specific destinations to visit or not to visit. The names of hotels and restaurants are usually not given, so the book does not have the practical usefulness of the book <u>Lonely Planet.</u> The book is also not a diary or travel journal. Thus, the overall structure of the book is not governed by chronological order or any painstaking slavishness in presenting one small detail after another.

To put it more clearly, I would have to say that this book is a series of impressions--sometimes witty, sometimes poignant, sometimes provocative--about New Zealand and Australia and the experiences Nancy and I had while touring these two wonderful countries. Because Nancy and I were on our own for nearly two months, there is a certain sense of adventure in the book. Adding this adventure to the fact that one of the spouses is blind creates a certain amount of inspiration in the book, although this is certainly a byproduct of the story rather than the prime motivation of the text.

The prime motivation of the text, I would have to say, is that if birds gotta sing, writers have to write. I would go beyond this and say that disabled people, when they can, even more strongly than most people, have a desire to share their stories and to speak out about their existence. In fact, nothing has surprised me more about my blindness than the fact that sometimes people actually ignore me! I have always been a very outgoing and entertaining personality, yet occasionally people that Nancy and I meet will refrain from talking to me and will have conversations with Nancy alone. In these conversations, these people insensitively refer to me in the third person! In addition, sometimes when I enter a room by myself, people seem to avoid me or ignore my presence. While this doesn't happen most of the time, when it does, it is shocking. Metaphorically, I sometimes feel like the character in Edgar Allen Poe's horror story "The Cask of Amontillado" who is bricked up inside a cavern and will never see the light of day again. Every time I am ignored or treated as a nonentity, I feel as if another brick is being mortared into place that will eventually shut me off from the reality of social communication. Writing strikes me as a chisel that I can use to break out of the bricks that are imprisoning me, and each page of text seems to me to be a step that I can climb up until I finally reach the light of day and find fully human acceptance.

But why did I choose Australia and New Zealand to forge my chisel? Why didn't I pick a country or two a lot more close to home? I have to confess that the blame most likely goes to Cornelius Vanderbilt. If it were not for this philanthropist, this book would probably be about Canada. Vanderbilt's sin was that he gave money to build libraries. One of these libraries was a fine library that was built in Bayonne, New Jersey, my hometown. When I was a sighted little boy, I used to toddle off to the Bayonne Public Library many times during the year. In fact, rainy days spent in the library are among my most pleasant childhood memories. There were always plenty of books--beautiful books. My favorites were nonfiction works that featured colored photographs. Half of the books would be text, and half would be pictures. I remember quite clearly the pleasure I got from the shiny covers. The paper, too, seemed very special as I turned from one page to another. I was most taken with books about the sea or places on the other side of the world. Octopuses, turtles, volcanoes, and pyramids all captured my imagination. However, my imagination went crazy when I finally saw a picture of a platypus. Then, of course, there were kangaroos, dingoes, and wombats. It was all too much--and it was all from Australia.

As soon as the time to travel made itself available in my life, my passion for Australia leapt from my dreams and into reality. With Nancy now retired, I had an expert traveling companion and a person whose love of new places and new experiences was even stronger than mine.

Part of Nancy's ability as a traveler lies in her powers of observation. One of her insights has consistently been proven true. As a person who regularly drove to conferences, Nancy observed how people in the front seats of cars often shared information about themselves in an open and free way that did not occur in other situations. In fact, she and I both take the position that a person can learn much more about a co-worker in the travels to a single conference than can be learned after months and months of working side by side.

This observation about the openly-communicating-traveler might be a good metaphor for this book. As the writer, I will be the driver of this communication vehicle. Sitting on my left (in New Zealand and Australia we drive on the other side) the reader in the passenger seat will hear my observations about what I experienced. In addition to passing the time, I hope that my observations will at times be interesting and occasionally entertaining. So, let's get ready to go. The passenger's windshield is clean; the vehicle is filled with energy; the destination is plotted and known. Oh, by the way, don't worry about the blind driver. He fancies that he is following the same path that has been driven by other blind drivers like Homer and Milton; only he is not driving as luxurious a vehicle.

THE TRIP THAT ALMOST WASN'T

The eighteenth-century poet Robert Burns once pointed out that the best laid plans of mice and men often do not come to fruition. My, he was certainly right! Nancy and I had planned our trip to Australia for several years. We had decided we wanted to go; we had decided we had the time to go, and we had decided that we had the money to go. We also were involving ourselves in the part of the trip that we really enjoyed; that is, the research and ruminations of about what would happen when we actually got to Australia. We also realized that Australia was a long way away--a long, long way away, and Nancy had decided that on this trip she could use a little assistance in planning the details and accommodations of our stay. She went on the Australian website and found a travel agency that called itself "All Over Down Under." As she clicked on the site, she discovered that the name of the travel director was a woman named Jeane (this is the spelling that she favors). When Nancy contacted Jeane, she quickly learned something that astonished both of us. Jeane lived in Marathon, New York, a small village only eleven miles or so from our house! While this was surprising, it was also quite convenient. Even more surprising than this was the fact that Jeane had seen me sing karaoke at the Three Bear's Inn in Marathon. I'm sure that this provided her with some insights and or speculations about what kind of character I was. However, this should not have given Jeane any idea about the nature of Nancy's personality. Nancy has never sung karaoke in public. More than this, she has never sung karaoke in private. Whether or not Jeane's decisions with regard to our accommodations were affected by karaoke, I don't know. However, after several meetings with Jeane all of our accommodations and all of the other practical matters related to our trip were taken care of before the end of November, 2006.

One thing remained for me to take care of before the trip. I had to stop this reflux problem I had--or I thought I had—that had given me a lot of concern. For several years the pain in my chest that occurred after I exercised following a meal seemed to be increasing. This had occurred so much so that I would put off taking a long walk until two or three hours had passed from the time I ate until the time I walked or exercised. It seemed the longer I waited to take a walk or exercise, the better I would feel. It also seemed that if I kept the strenuous nature of the exercise down and maintained a good time distance from the eating of a meal, my pain would not appear or would be relatively mild. Although I'm usually slow to take medications and wait until such medications were absolutely necessary, I found myself becoming more and more aggressive with the kinds of medications I would grab to stop this reflux pain. Like a child at a party where there are numerous M&M cups available for the taking, I would pop Gaviscon, Pepcid-AC and any other over the counter medicine into my mouth if it promised in its commercials that such intake of the product would relieve the symptoms of the reflux. The pain was so annoying that I would even risk the usual side effects in order to combat the pain. I was ready to experience dry mouth, mild headache, diarrhea, constipation, and even a runny nose if the pain relievers would work. By the way, I have a standard rule of thumb for the efficacy of drugs, whether they are bought over the counter or are prescription. If the medicine I am taking does not have a side effect of diarrhea, it is probably a placebo.

Despite consuming every anti-reflux medicine created since 1920, I found nothing I could count on and complained to my physician that I had to do something. She listened attentively to my complaints, and because I rarely complained about anything at the doctor's office except the fact they didn't wait long enough to get all my clothing off to weigh me, she took my complaint very seriously. Eventually we agreed that I might want to pursue an outpatient surgical procedure that promised relief from reflux by going to the source. As the fall of 2006 was winding down, my doctor and I made plans to have me admitted to a hospital in Syracuse to have this minor procedure done. The procedure would occasion me to stay overnight. This would be my first overnight in a hospital ever.

However, at my regular physical in early December my doctor gave me some surprising news. She felt somewhat uneasy about this overnight procedure in January and went back and looked at a heart monitor I had worn for 24 hours at a previous physical. As she poured over the results of that heart monitoring, she noticed a little something. Most of us know that when a doctor finds this "little something," something is indeed up. She comforted me by saying that it was probably nothing, but I was not so sure it was going to be nothing. In any event she told me she had scheduled a stress test just to see if my heart was working as it should. I'll never forget what happened on Friday, December 15, 2006 when I showed up for the stress test.

I arrived ready to beat this test back. I am, if nothing else, a rather competitive person. I had my running shorts on and was ready to show that I was still in pretty good shape. I hadn't eaten much, so I thought the reflux thing might not be much of a factor. When the cardiologist got me on the stress treadmill, I couldn't believe how fast he upped the ante! I guess he was pretty competitive too. Within seconds of the treadmill being turned on, the incline was probably similar to the difficulty of the Hillary Step on Mt. Everest. In addition, the speed was easily five miles an hour, and it was only a matter of time before my face changed from pink to red to purple and the sweat began to fall from my body. The pain somewhat surprised me; there was very little, and then there was plenty. I said uncle in as many languages as I knew and the doctor took me and seated me on the bed. The echo devices were monitoring very quickly what was happening in my heart. I think the cardiologist got a little scared by what he saw, and he asked me if I was in pain. When I was able to sit upright and stop holding my side, I said I was. That's when I knew I was in real trouble. He slipped me a couple of nitroglycerine tablets and told me to put them under my tongue. Nitroglycerine tablets! I knew that these were only given to people that have heart problems. I didn't want to have a heart problem. Yet, I had serious pain; I had nitroglycerine tablets melting under my tongue, and I had a cardiologist telling that he was going to call up a major hospital in Syracuse to take care of me.

The doctor called St. Joseph's Hospital in Syracuse--a hospital known for its cardiac care and heart surgery. Within 2 minutes he had a room scheduled for me on Monday the 18th of December. The nitroglycerine had exploded a lot of myths about myself. I wasn't immortal; I couldn't just walk it off, and it wasn't a sure thing to go to Australia. I felt glad about being blind because I didn't have to look into my wife's eyes. If I had, I'm sure we both would have formed the word disappointment from my iris to hers and her iris to mine as we looked at each other and wondered if our plans for a trip to Australia had just been destroyed by a small pair of nitroglycerine tablets.

As I left the treatment room of the hospital, the doctor advised me to take it easy over the weekend. This was an amazing comment. Here I was with some kind of obvious heart trouble. Yet, somehow I was supposed to be relaxed over the weekend. Obviously, he didn't want me to do any physical activity, but how I was going to be able to take it easy was beyond my comprehension. I wondered to myself if I could overdo taking my own pulse. I would obviously want to stay in touch with how my heart was doing and make sure it kept on pumping. I guess I also assumed that it was now too late to consume health bestowing benefits of fish as my main meal choice for all of my meals during the next several days. Although I took some solace in the fact that I had been eating in a pretty healthy way over the last fifteen years and had a pretty energetic lifestyle with lots of exercise, I did have moments of regret for those cheeseburgers that had populated my life in my twenties and thirties as well as the salted peanuts that I craved so often. My problem was genetic, and I knew it, but this fact did not enable me to "take it easy".

I certainly felt relieved when I arrived at the hospital on Monday. If something were going to happen to me, I couldn't imagine a better place where it might happen than St. Joseph's Hospital in Syracuse. I was scheduled for an angiogram and perhaps the placement of a stent if what the camera showed for my heart made a stent a possible treatment. As I waited in the hospital's staging area, I was able to listen to people dealing with their stress in lots of different ways. One youngish fellow in his fifties kept shouting out, "Crack me open" as he went from the bathroom back to his bed and back to the bathroom again and again and again. He was obviously very nervous and perhaps felt a great deal of guilt since it was very clear that he had been a smoker for his entire life.

Finally, I was taken to the operating suite where as usual in the modern world, I might as well had been beamed up to a flying saucer. Even though I couldn't see them clearly, I knew there were a bank of computers on one wall that were being monitored by one technician as well as numerous other devices including the moveable table that allowed the operating physician to look carefully at the photograph that the miniature camera was taking under his direction. The rock and roll music a little too softly in the background did provide a little comfort although I would have preferred to hear the lyrics a little more clearly. The discomfort of the procedure wasn't bad at all although it was a new kind of pain that I hadn't felt before. The procedure was supposed to take about an hour and a half to perhaps two hours, and when mine ended after only about a half an hour or thirty-five minutes, I knew something was wrong.

When I got back to the staging area again, Nancy was already there and she had already shared with the doctors the bad news. The camera showed that the blood vessels going to my heart were significantly blocked. The one thing keeping me going happened to be those collateral blood vessels that developed through years of intense exercise. There was no possibility of using stents in this situation and so a surgeon by the name of Dr. Randy Green told me I was scheduled on that Friday for bypass surgery. All of a sudden, the sounds of a *didgeridoo* had changed to the silence of the *didgeri-don't*. My heart, deprived of a normal flow of blood, could still sink by hearing the news of the quadruple bypass surgery. Surely now, I thought, the idea of a spring visit to Australia seemed out of the question. However, my mind soon changed. I had several days to wait before the drugs wore off that had thinned my blood so that it wouldn't clot. Now that I was about to undergo open heart surgery, I needed my blood to clot for all it was worth. I had in effect another three days to "take it easy." One part of me kept pretty focused on rooting for me not to have a heart attack. I hadn't had one and, my recovery would be greatly enhanced and advanced if I did not suffer one three days before my surgery. If I could get to Friday and have the operation, I would have had blood flow restored to a healthy heart. This would be a great thing. It would, of course, perhaps make it possible for me to make the trip I so longed to take.

Well, the gods were with me, and Dr. Green and his people did a spectacular job in my operation. I was surprised by the lack of pain following such an incredible operation. Although I was taking pain-killing drugs, my level of pain never got past 2 out of 10. What did get to me was the overwhelming weakness I felt after the operation. The nurses kept after me to keep moving and to keep trying to get back to normal as quickly as physically possible. Indeed the next day I was sitting up and even took a couple of steps to get into a chair near my bed. I am also quite proud of the fact that when I was awakened after being put in intensive care, the first thing I did to prove to the nurse that I was still in good enough shape was to recite Shakespeare's sonnet "When in Disgrace" to show I still had my mental capacity well in order.

A few days later when I was released from the hospital, I must admit that Australia was a long way off. I was having trouble walking from my bed to the bathroom. It seemed a major achievement to take a seat on the toilet. Comparing this to a ten thousand mile journey made me pause about my optimistic view of the future. Yet the human body is an amazing machine. From ten minutes of walking in my hallway, I was soon walking with Nancy for a half hour on the streets in my neighborhood so that within a month I was walking two miles everyday at about a three mile per hour pace.

Although my visiting nurse had said I still had a possibility of going to Australia, the real answer would come with my visit to my surgeon January 22nd. As I sat in his waiting room, I wondered what he would say. Nancy and I were first in the waiting room and we critically examined all of the patients that came after us. Most of them were twenty years older than I was, and the colors of their faces were not as healthy as mine. In addition, many of them were carrying oxygen bottles or were having trouble sitting up. In an odd way I thought this helped my case. Surely when the doctor came into his office and peeked into his waiting room, he would think to himself, "Who is the pick of the litter in this room?" or "Who is the most likely to return most quickly to normal life?" In fact, when I saw the doctor, he seemed pretty pleased to see me. He had just come from an extra-long operation where he had to work very feverishly to save a life. Sitting there talking to me seemed like easy business. He came over and examined me in the way that doctors do when the patient wonders what they actually can find out just with that short listen to one's heart, but he seemed pleased with what he heard. After he explained that I looked good and that my heart sounded fine, I responded that I was feeling good, but I had to ask him a question. This was the big moment. "Doctor, what do you think about me going to Australia?" I asked. After a moment's pause he responded with words that I will never forget. He told me that when he operated on me, he did it to give me twenty years more of a vibrant exciting life. He said going to Australia was a vibrant and exciting thing to do. He then summed it up with just those wonderful three words, "Go to Australia."

With these words ringing in our ears, Nancy and I left in a very happy mood from Dr. Green's office. We went to a mall, walked around and celebrated with a dinner. By this time I was beginning to feel very tired from what had been a very exciting day, and I realized my decision to go to Australia was going to take some fortitude and commitment on my part if the trip was to be successful. Yet it was a commitment I embraced, and we left Cortland on February 22nd —exactly two months after my surgery. We did so with confidence that not only would we have a trip that we would enjoy, but one we would enjoy in a very special and intense way.

NOT SIGHTSEEING BUT SITED BEING

For sighted people, traveling without vision must seem like a pointless exercise. However, a quick series of reflections prove that this is not the case. I think that most people would realize that certainly the blind traveler is going to get a lot of satisfaction from sampling the food and, of course, having conversations with others at mealtimes. For me, even exploring new hotels and motel rooms provides an interesting diversion. In addition, there is always the sense that when one is traveling one is alive. I feel that I am a character in a novel as I make my way across the Mediterranean or across the frontiers of the Australian continent. Nonetheless, there are significant moments that stand out in my mind that perhaps will make it clear what kind of joy and excitement travel can bring even to one who is dealing with blindness. What I would like to do, therefore, is to present some of the experiences I had in New Zealand and Australia that will bring the point home that blind travel can be high travel.

Climbing Mount Victoria

With 48 dormant and extinct volcanic craters, Auckland is a city of peaks. These peaks--more appropriately, volcanic vents--do not challenge the height of Mt. Everest at 29,028 feet. Nonetheless, they do provide an interesting topographical feature that certainly grabs the attention of every tourist to this wonderful city. When Nancy and I took a ferry across the harbor, we arrived at one of these peaks--Mt. Victoria. Mt. Victoria is less than 300 feet high; however, since it is a volcanic crater, the sides are rather steep. When Nancy decided that she wanted to get to the top of one of these vents, a dormant cone named Mt. Victoria, I was outwardly eager to join her although inwardly I felt a tinge of anxiety about the prospect of the climb. It had been just a little more than two months since I had my quadruple bypass surgery. To be sure, I had been working out quite aggressively, but the thought of moving my body up the vertical slope of a crater seemed a challenge. There was a roadway that snaked around the crater so that cars could get to the top, and this gave me some confidence that the journey would not be too bad. As we climbed up, I assessed my physiology at every step. About a third of the way up, I began to relax. Although the climb was somewhat strenuous, it did not seem to threaten my very life. At about this point, Nancy decided that we needed to go off the roadway and take a shortcut. She had been monitoring my breathing and my pace. With both showing no significant signs of stress or fatigue, she concluded that taking a shortcut was well within my capabilities. We were now on dirt, and the ascent was a bit more vertical, but it would save time. As the dirt gave way under my feet, I found it necessary to get on all fours in order to scramble up the steep sides of the crater. Making the way more interesting was the fact that on all fours I had to duck under the branches of several trees. As I scrambled and struggled in the brush, I thought about how only two months before it had taken a nurse to take me the ten feet from my bed to a chair in my hospital room. Now, I was climbing a mountain! When we finally reconnected with the automobile road, I felt a sense of elation. I had conquered the hardest part of the ascent. Although we had a considerable way to go to get to the top, the remaining climb seemed a lot easier than what I had already traversed. When we finally got to the top, I couldn't help but wonder whether I could get a flag to plant on the top of Mt. Victoria. It wouldn't be a flag to represent a country; it would be a flag representing my growth and confidence. As my breathing and heart rate slowed down, I became sure that my trip to New Zealand and Australia would be an experience I could look forward to with confidence and anticipation.

THE PATH TO HUKA FALLS

The Waikato River is the longest river in New Zealand. At Huka Falls the river makes a spectacular descent on its way eventually to Lake Taupo. To reach these falls, a path was constructed that is parallel to the river. As a trail, this path was rated as "easy" by park officials. Nancy and I read this with interest as we glanced at the information board in the car park to decide whether or not we wanted to take a hike up this trail. I must say, however, that "easy" to a New Zealander is different from what the word "easy" means to an American. In New Zealand an easy trail is one that does not require mountaineering equipment. As the trail to Huka Falls would demonstrate, it doesn't make any difference how steep the ascent is or how long the climb is. As long as mountainering equipment is not required, the path is easy. I can only assume that a "moderate" path would be one where mountaineering equipment was required, but an individual would be able to make the climb by himself. Now a "difficult" path or trail would be one where not only mountaineering equipment would be required, but there also would be a need to climb with others and be connected to them with security ropes. However, when Nancy and I began our hike on the trail to Huka Falls, we had not yet realized the kind of system the New Zealanders were using. We started off with enthusiasm. The river churned in rapids near us; the path was wide and level. Then we began a gentle climb, and the river was no longer at our side. Suddenly, the climb became steep, quite steep. I assumed that this was just an aberration and that this was something that would not be repeated. At the top of the aberration we descended quite steeply down the other side. From this point on, I began to feel that I was walking the rails of a roller coaster rather than taking a leisurely hike on an "easy" path. The aberration became the norm and the degree of steepness became more and more severe. As we descended from the top of the rolling hills, it sometimes became difficult for us to hold our feet in place. We almost became dirt skiers in our sneakers. There are certain things I notice when a hiking path becomes unexpectedly steep. In the first place, the pacing of people begins to vary greatly. As a result, Nancy and I would have to pass slower hikers or be passed by those who were faster than we were. Heavy breathing becomes quite noticeable as each group is encountered. Finally, conversation tends to cease--not only between Nancy and me but between all the groups of the hikers who come by. However, there was one thing I'll never forget. That is the presence of strollers with infants or toddlers in them. New Zealand hikers are a different breed. They will not be put off by steepness; they will take their children and their strollers with them wherever the sign says "easy-"-even if that "easy" has a very different meaning in the great islands down-under.

Nancy and I pressed on for several kilometers, but as we walked, we began to realize we were not going to walk all the way to the falls. Nancy pointed out to me that some of the hikers coming back down the path seemed quite bedraggled, and they were thirty years younger than we were. The climb up to Mt. Victoria had been steep--sometimes as steep as this path, but it was short. We knew on the Huka path that we would have to go back the same way we came. This meant that we would have to go up and down the very steep places we had already conquered. It was not just the matter of going down; it was a matter of going up and down. So, when we reached the rest area, we decided to turn back. We were at least three kilometers from our car--far enough on this type of terrain.

When I got back to the car, I was tired but elated. Although I was perspiring, I was still in good physical shape. I had pressed my body into another demanding physical challenge, and I had held up fine. I had also gained a great sense of participation with the other hikers on the trail. I had exerted my body, smelled the vegetation, heard the sounds of the birds and other animals in the forest, and most of all, enjoyed the sounds of the rushing water near me. It had been a good morning, and I was ready for lunch.

WALKING THE SYDNEY HARBOR BRIDGE

When I was a boy, the two longest steel-arch bridges in the world were the Bayonne Bridge and the Sydney Harbor Bridge. The Bayonne Bridge was 504 meters long and spanned the Kill Van Kull that separates Bayonne, New Jersey from Staten Island, New York. Besides the fact that the Bayonne Bridge was my hometown bridge, it was also a bridge that my grandfather, Joseph, had helped to build. He was an ironworker and found good employment in building that remarkable structure. There is also a quite tragic side to my family with the bridge. My uncle Roscoe's wife was the first woman to commit suicide from that bridge. The Sydney Harbor Bridge was only slightly shorter than the Bayonne Bridge. In fact, it was only one meter shorter at 503 meters. Yet to say that the Sydney Harbor Bridge was a smaller bridge belies the reality. The Bayonne Bridge has only two narrow lanes in both directions and a small sidewalk for pedestrians. The Sydney Harbor Bridge, on the other hand, has three broad lanes in each direction as well as railroad tracks and a fairly wide pedestrian walkway. The Bayonne Bridge has a certain grace to it; the Harbor Bridge shouts out its grandeur.

I remember walking across the Bayonne Bridge when I was a boy. I was perhaps eleven or twelve years old and walked over the bridge with my brother and a few friends. We had our bicycles with us and walked across the bridge to travel to the Staten Island Zoo. For us, it was like walking to another country. Part of the magic of the trip was the tremendous height over the water we experienced when we got to the apex of the bridge. The boat traffic below us looked incredibly small as we watched large ocean freighters glide beneath our feet. I recall that the high winds and unreal atmosphere on the bridge made me wonder at the ability of men who were able to build such a structure. When I used to look at photographs of the Sydney Harbor Bridge, I felt a kinship and familiarity because of its steel-arch structure. As Nancy and I planned our trip to Australia, one thing I knew I wanted to do was walk across the bridge.

We were lucky when we visited Sydney because it was in the midst of its celebration of the seventy-fifth anniversary of the bridge. As an icon for not only Sydney but for Australia as well, the bridge was everywhere--on tee shirts, on coffee cups, on posters, and, of course, just about on every postcard.

It indeed was an exciting day when we took off for the bridge. It was a typically beautiful day in Sydney-- the winds were light; the sky was blue; and the temperature was about 75 degrees. Finding the stairs to the bridge's roadway took quite a bit of time, but once we were on the sidewalk surface, the walk was quite exhilarating. The rise on the sidewalk as we reached the apex of the arch of the roadway was quite small and presented no serious physical exertion. The impact on my senses was tremendously exciting. As I walked along the bridge, the sounds of life and a vibrant harbor were everywhere. I certainly could hear quite strongly sounds of busy traffic in both directions that were using the bridge. These sounds were punctuated by percussion of tires when the tires would hit the metal of the expansion joints that were part of the roadway. Four cylinder motors and large diesel engines shouted for my attention. Below and above me I could hear the sounds of propeller-driven aircraft that were helping tourists get a better view of Sydney Harbor. Some of the planes passed under the bridge; others soared above it. Occasionally, a ferry horn would announce its presence in the cacophony of commercial activity that is the Sydney Harbor. In the background to this symphony of sound, the wind provided a steady base beat as it moved between the bodies of water that the bridge had conquered.

But sound was not my only experience. My feet could feel the gentle rise of the sidewalk as Nancy and I proceeded along our path. When a train sought to cross the bridge, I could feel the rumblings beneath my feet. These rumblings were in addition to the constant mini-jolts I felt when cars and trucks rode over an expansion joint. My body began to perspire as I continued walking and the wind on one side of my body chilled me slightly while the warm sun on the other side of my body counteracted this chill with the full benefit of the sun's warmth. In addition to tactile sensations, the bridge also provided stimuli for my sense of smell. When the bridge soared over land, it often was positioned above the rising smells of the numerous kitchens serving the Circular Quay. Since the time was approaching the lunch hour, the smells were various, fantastic, and enticing. The variety of cuisine that is a hallmark of Sydney was certainly evident in the food fragrances that rose to our nostrils as Nancy and I continued our walk.

Walking the Sydney Bridge was thrilling. Because I had seen the bridge and harbor when I was younger in various travel books, I had a virtual reality in my mind's eye of what the bridge looked like and what the harbor looked like. When I was on the bridge, all of my other senses became totally involved. Having a disability often means isolation, yet here I was with the love of my life being involved in a total way with one of the great structures of the world and surely one of the great cities of the planet.

UPLIFTING FALLS

If nothing else, I am a person of paradox. Though I am an academic and thinker, I am very physical. I love to walk and to lift weights, to use my body as well as my mind. In addition, my tastes in entertainment often seem contradictory. I can enjoy listening to a Shakespearean play and then put on Them, a movie about giant ants terrorizing Los Angeles. I can also listen to an operatic aria and then make a selection that takes me back to rock and roll. It is no surprise then that as this book illustrates, I am not comfortable with the typical identity of the disabled or blind person. I want to be the hero of a novel, the star of my own movie. The trip that Nancy and I took to Wentworth Falls in the Blue Mountains outside of Sydney fits in this vein. Nancy had seen the Falls touted as one of the attractions as she consulted her guidebook. She asked me if I was interested in going there. She was concerned that perhaps the Falls would not interest me much since, although it had a possible aural component if a thunderous amount of water might be creating a powerful sound, it was largely a visual experience. I, however, thought that it might also include some kind of walk, and so I was glad to go. Indeed, in order to get to the Falls we did have to take a walk, but this walk was predominantly a winding set of stairs. When I say a set of stairs, perhaps I am giving the wrong idea. A "set" implies a regularity of construction, and this was certainly not the case with the steep, wood-filled path down to the Falls. The steps were usually made of timbers, but these were of various heights--approximately 14 inches high to perhaps 4 inches high. These steps, of course, would turn and move as the path did. Making things more interesting were drainage ditches that would cut across the path at various points. Sometimes two or three steps of various heights would be very close together; the steps would be separated--sometimes by a regular distance, sometimes by an irregular distance. The wild card would be the drainage ditches. Now, for a blind person, steps are not necessarily a problem. If the steps are regular size and space, a blind person can negotiate them quite easily. For that matter, escalators do not impose a particular problem for a blind person although many people think so. I remember a few years ago how I startled people by handling the escalators in a large hotel quite naturally and easily even though some of my sighted friends were having some difficulty using them because of some problems with their trifocals. One thing that is obvious is that going down stairs is much riskier than going up stairs. The culprit of course is gravity.

When Nancy and I began descending the stairs, I was quite

enthusiastic about the potential walk. A park sign had indicated that the walk would take about 20 minutes each way to get to the Falls. This seemed to me about the right amount of time for a stimulating physical adventure of about forty minutes. It was a humid day, and the sun had been shining, so Nancy and I were only dressed in tee shirts and shorts. As Nancy and I descended the stairs and proceeded along the path, I vigorously employed my cane as an antenna of ambulation. I moved it briskly and variously so that I could ascertain the kind of step that I was approaching. In addition, Nancy called out the presence of the numerous drainage ditches as they came along. The path at times was steeper than we had anticipated. Both of us focused quite strongly on the details of the steps so that gravity would not make his presence known in a fall that could be catastrophic. I could hear in people's voices coming up the steps a sense of surprise as they greeted us along the path. I'm sure they were surprised that a blind person would make such a journey down such a steep and perhaps, difficult path.

I was beginning to lose interest in the activity after we had been traveling for about 25 minutes. Almost on cue, Nancy announced that we were just about at the bottom of the path and she could see the Falls in the distance. Just at this point, the skies opened up and the rains began to fall in earnest. With all the talk about drought and the morning sunshine, Nancy and I did not expect this. Clearly, neither of us had anything but the shirts on our backs to protect us from the rain. I don't remember a time in my life that I was forced to stand in the rain without any protection. However, we were able to innovate and adapt. Nancy and I crowded under a plant that had particularly broad leaves. In our usually hopeful way, we expected the rain to last only for a short time. The leaves on the plant did indeed break the impact of the rain; although we did get wet we could certainly endure. After about ten minutes, the rain ceased. Nancy went off to view the Falls and I remained at the bottom of the path and enjoyed a conversation with an Australian hiker.

The climb back up the path was more strenuous, of course, but in many ways it was easier. If I fell on the way back up, I might skin my knee and get a little muddy but wouldn't break an arm or a leg. I also enjoyed the thought that I was exercising my heart in a positive way. The glass of confidence that I had begun to fill at Mt. Victoria and Huka

River was now rising to the full. This sense of elation gave a spring to my step, and although we were climbing uphill, the time it took us to reach the car park was about the same as it was going down.

Our walk to Wentworth Falls had become another highlight of the trip. I enjoyed conquering the fear that the treacherous downhill steps had created. I also felt one with nature, having endured a downpour without protection probably the first time in my life. Also I had gotten another walker's high from finishing a strenuous uphill walk. Perhaps most of all, I enjoyed the thought that I accompanied Nancy to something she wanted to see and made it not just a singular experience for her but an experience for me that we shared together.

REMARKABLE ROCKS

Another site that really invigorated me was the site of Remarkable Rocks in the National Park on Kangaroo Island southwest of Adelaide. This was the only time that Nancy and I were on a tour. It was a small two-night tour on Kangaroo Island, a place noted for its abundant wildlife.

While the wildlife had indeed been the promised treat of the tour, the program of events included a visit to the Remarkable Rocks. When Nancy read to me that we would be visiting some rocks, I must say that I was not totally convinced that this was a trip I wanted to make. However, since the tour bus would be gone most of the day, I felt that a short stop at a bunch of rocks would probably be tolerable. I became eventually very glad that I had made this decision.

When we arrived at the rocks, the wind was blowing across the sea at about 60 miles per hour. Unimpeded by any land, the winds blew across a thousand miles of open ocean that ended at Antarctica. As we left the bus, Nancy told me that a series of boardwalks would take us to the rocks. They were large bowling balls of granite that were each the size of a small house. Each boulder was situated on a rounded piece of granite. As we left the boardwalk and walked on the granite base, I began to hold Nancy's arm much more tightly. Walking up a rounded surface has never been one of my favorite things, and being buffeted by such strong winds made the experience even more frightening. As I tapped with my cane against the surface of the stone, I realized how puny my little cane was. I also realized how puny I was. As we approached the gigantic bowling ball of our choice, I surmised that I was mostly underneath it. As my arms went up I could feel the granite above and over me. At this point, I also began to think about the sea. Those fierce winds were doing more than blowing air; they were raising massive waves. These swells were now about 20 feet high, and they were crashing into the base of the granite that supported the Remarkable Rocks. I could feel the gargantuan thud of each wave as it ended its trip to the shore. These rocks might be remarkable, but what I began to think that was more remarkable was the fact that I was standing under tons of stone—stone that was being buffeted by gale-force winds and nudged to move by a sea that was powerful and insistent.

Strangely enough, I was quite exhilarated to be in this dangerous position, but my exhilaration had a limited lifespan. I began to think of longer life spans, especially my own. I told Nancy that I had about as much fun as I could endure, so let's get the heck out of here. As we crossed the road and got back to the bus, Nancy went on another hike to view some seals on a beach below us. I sat calmly on a bench nicely situated for tourists. With no rocks hanging over my head and a comfortable place to sit, I put aside my usual desire for hiking and activity as I enjoyed a moment of sedentary safety.

SPIRES THAT TOOK ME HIGHER

Most tourists that spend more than a month in Europe inevitably say, "If I ever see another cathedral, I don't think I'll shed a tear." The reason for this is that Europe is absolutely stuffed with cathedrals, some of these having histories that go back in time nearly a thousand years. Each cathedral has a history that is rich in religious information, political background, and of course, artistic richness. Each city and village is also very proud of its cathedral, so these edifices are required visiting for any tourist who visits a European community. With its relatively short European history of about two hundred and forty years and a relatively small population, Australia does not have the density of houses of worship that is typical in Europe; however, Australia does have some cathedrals and churches, and the Australians are just as proud of these places of worship as any European. For Nancy and me, visits to some of these churches turned out to be much more than a religious observation on Sunday.

St. Monica's Cathedral in Cairns is a case in point. When Nancy and I decided to attend church on this particular Sunday, we had no idea what the church would be like. However, when we entered the church Nancy was spellbound by the stain glass windows that were all around the church. These windows sent a religious message through an extremely colorful presentation of the natural world. Fishes and sea creatures, coral reefs, mountains and volcanoes, and other natural wonders were all part of God's greatness that caught the eye of the visitor in a way that was new and exciting. Of course, while I enjoyed sharing Nancy's excitement about the windows, I was not able to enjoy her vision of them. For me, the excitement came in other areas. As a member of a church choir, I enjoy singing the hymns of my faith. One of the special things about being a Roman Catholic is that the services around the world are essentially the same. Indeed many of the hymns are identical whether one is in Cortland, New York or Wales or Cairns, Australia. On this particular Sunday there were several hymns that I had memorized so that I was able to join in the singing with great gusto. My voice is a gift from God, and I do enjoy utilizing it. Afterwards, Nancy told me that when I began to sing, many of the people around me turned to see who had brought this unusual voice into the church. I really enjoy it when people look at me not in terms of my having a deficit but possessing a wonderful gift.

On Palm Sunday in Adelaide, Nancy and I had a much different kind of experience. We found a church in town and had entered only to discover that this particular Mass was going to be entirely said in Croatian. Obviously, there was a significant Croatian population in Adelaide. Nancy asked me if I wanted to hear Mass in Croatian, and I decided that it would be an interesting change of pace. Although there were many more words in the liturgy this particular day since the Passion was read as the Gospel, there were only a few words that I was able to pick out. The proper name for Peter was identifiable during the Gospel reading. After Mass, as announcements were read I was also able to pick out the word picnic. Nonetheless, the liturgy still was familiar. By our responses and movements in the pew, I had the sense of the precise point in the liturgy that we were celebrating at just about each and every moment. Furthermore, there were a couple things of interest in the physical sense of the church itself. Because palms actually grow in this region, the church was full of palm branches secured to all of the columns in the church. When Nancy and I came back from Communion, we almost had to cut our way through a jungle of palms that were attached to the column that was at the edge of our pew. Another interesting element of this church was that there were no kneelers. The floor was carpeted, and the congregation was expected to kneel on the floor. Since my knees are in pretty good shape, I enjoyed this bit of mortification.

At Brisbane, Nancy and I once again attended a cathedral. The memorable impression from this grand church was the music. The choir director must have had an incredibly strong musical background as well as very strong opinions about what church music could and should sound like. In this case the usual traditions did not rule. The musical selections sounded much more like pieces from <u>Les Miserables</u> than from any common listing of choral hymns. I marveled that his choir could even come close to what the conductor was expecting of them. I certainly did not sing along.

The final cathedral that I'd like to mention would be St. Mary's in Sydney. Since it is the cathedral in the nation's largest city, it is not surprising that St. Mary's is a magnificent building set off on a tremendously large piece of land. On the Sunday we visited St. Mary's, there was also an Irish festival going on across the street. As Nancy and I passed through the park and the festival, we were struck by the behavior of the festival-goers at this relatively late point in the day. Our Mass was a 5:00 P.M. affair. Many of the festival-goers were quite intoxicated at this time. As this was a common festival setting, certain physical arrangements had been made to accommodate the drinking of alcoholic beverages. For example, large chain-link fences were setup to enclose the sites for the distribution of alcohol. From my blind perspective it almost seemed that the intoxicated were caged within these high chain-link fences. As Nancy and I crossed the street to enter into the cathedral, a very loud Irish rock band was just taking the stage at the festival. Once inside the church, I was struck by the contrast. At the festival I had heard the slurred and incoherent ramblings of drunks punctuated by shouts of anger as well as by hysterical shrieks of laughter.

To be sure, there were as many people happy as there were people unhappy, but the social filters had clearly been discarded and thrown into a river of alcohol. In the church the congregation was subdued and meditative. The mood was peaceful. The music that surrounded all of the activity was similar to Gregorian chant. Pensiveness, peace, prayer and perspective seemed the order of the day. Yet, even as the liturgy moved on, I could still hear bits of the Irish rock band filtering into the church. The wailing guitars, muddled words and musical screams from the lead singer intruded upon the solemnity of the religious service and into my ears. However, all this did was underscore the differences in human behavior and to make a moral point in my mind that a printed catechism would never do.

Thus it is clear to me that taking time out for religion on Sunday does not interrupt the travel experience. Indeed, for me as a blind man, the Sunday service provides many opportunities not only to reflect about my relationship with the deity, but also to experience unique elements of worship that are part of the cultural landscape of the places I visited.

THE BEACH WAS A BALL

When I was a child, visits to the Jersey Shore were the highlights of summer activities. My brother Chris and I loved to body surf, and we were quite good at it. We would often spend up to six hours doing this activity; only exhaustion could get us out of the water. One particular occasion that stands out in my memory occurred after a hurricane just touched New Jersey. As we looked along the shore, we could see several houses damaged by the strong surf. This day the sun was partially out, and the surf was still very high under the influence of the offshore hurricane. My brother and I were young teenagers at the time and fairly good swimmers. As a result, we had no qualms about entering this rough surf. It was about 1960 then, and rugged individualism still reigned in America; the nanny state was still a couple of decades away. I'm sure that if the same conditions existed today that lifeguards would keep everyone from getting into the water. But we were still in the days of freedom, choice and individual responsibility and Chris and I enjoyed our freedom to the fullest. We rode the waves in as never before. I remember clearly several occasions when I could get my body into the curl of a large wave so that my torso was actually outside of the wave as I was propelled with great velocity towards the shore. The crashing of the wave on the sand was always a turbulent moment, but my young body was flexible and strong and I was able to tumble nicely without hurting myself.

With such a tradition of sand and surf in my background, I looked forward to visiting Australia--a beach country if there ever was one. Even though I was no longer a sighted teenager, I still was interested in visiting numerous beaches. However, I wasn't all that enthusiastic about getting in the water. Since the onset of my blindness, I have developed a caution that usually comes with age and some misgivings about being in the water. Jellyfish and sharks were things that people could see. I knew that I wouldn't know about them until it was too late. My reading about the box jellyfish in particular caused me deep concern. A tangle with one of these deadly creatures would not just inconvenience me, it would kill me! In addition, both Bondi and Manly beaches were filled with various kinds of human activity. Surfers of all types--some on regular surfboards, some on boogie boards, and some bodysurfing--were all enjoying themselves in very busy surf. There was just too much action for me to feel comfortable in the water. Nonetheless, these beautiful beaches still had plenty of sand, the vibrant sounds of human happiness, and a penetrating connection to my happy past. While I lay on the sand and enjoyed the warmth of the sun, Nancy--more courageous than I--frolicked in the surf. Even a whack on the forehead from an errant boogie board did not stop her enjoyment. As I enjoyed the experience, I also envied the residents of Sydney. Manly Beach is a treasure that is quite amazing in its convenience to the city. A short ferry ride from Sydney puts one on the beach in less than a half hour. There isn't the regular congestion of the Garden State Parkway and the terrible delays that can occur when an accident intensifies this congestion. The ferries run all day, and the trip itself across the Sydney Harbor is a magnificent experience in itself.

The astonishing thing is that all of the large cities in Australia have their beaches--beautiful beaches--that are extremely easy to reach by public transportation. In fact, the state of Queensland is over a 1000 miles of sandy beaches! On the Gold Coast in Queensland Nancy and I visited a place that has achieved legendary status from beach goers—Surfers' Paradise. The phrase "Surfers' Paradise" is not merely descriptive; it is the actual name of a municipality. As the story goes, the place had a rather boring name in the 1930s. The town fathers wanted to increase tourism in the area. What better way could be found to increase tourism than to make the name itself an advertising slogan! Thus, Surfers' Paradise became the official name of this particular town. It is indeed a paradise for surfers. It includes a magnificent beach and many restaurants, bars and accommodations to handle anyone who wants to spend a week in the sun on this marvelous coast. Today some travel writers and Australians feel the Gold Coast is too gaudy and too overbuilt. However, with my New Jersey background, I found the Gold Coast rather tasteful and understated.

The ability to visit the wonderful beaches of Australia brought me back to the wonderful days of my childhood. While I was not able to do all the things that I did then, I was able to enjoy my memories and through my senses of touch and hearing to relive a wonderful part of my past as I enjoyed one of the assets of Australia that make it a excellent place to visit.

STARRING IN SYDNEY

I am a terrible spectator. I don't want to experience life vicariously; I want to experience it myself vibrantly. This sometimes might make me seem odd to people who have formulated ideas about what a blind person should be like. For some, the disabled need to be on a shelf, perhaps in a special case, so that they don't injure themselves. Unfortunately, there are some disabled that fall into this trap, yet there are others who provide tremendous inspiration for others as well as excitement in their own lives by the things they do. Blind people run casino empires and control professional basketball franchises. A blind person has summited Mt. Everest and another has conquered the several thousand miles of the Appalachian Trail. I've thrown my lot into this latter group. I want to be a star in my own movie. I guess there is some vanity in this, but there is also a tremendous amount of motivation. When I engage in life, I am happy. I don't need Dr. Phil to tell me that this engagement of life is not associated with depression.

In my movie, there are, of course, action scenes, and some of them have already been described in this book. In addition, there are also romantic scenes; one of them will be described right now. Nancy and I were in the final hours of the Australian movie. We were staying in the section of Sydney called The Rocks, a place close to Circular Quay on Sydney Harbor. Our final day included ferry rides, a visit to the beach, and some restaurants and shopping. Now it was evening. The fireworks display had just ended and the smells of the cuisines of all types of restaurants were invitingly flowing in the warm harbor air. Exotic music drifted by from a nearby bistro, and I asked Nancy if there was a bench we could sit on.

As we sat down, I could imagine how the lights around the harbor were adding to this romantic scene. The bridge and the opera house were very well lit, and the navigational lights of the boats in the harbor sprinkled further illumination upon the scene like tiny sparkling bulbs on a maritime Christmas tree. I placed my arm around Nancy and contemplated how lucky I was. Here I had a companion who not only had a lot of nerve but was also highly well read, quite beautiful and able to handle a 22-foot motor home for over 2000 kilometers. There aren't a lot of women like her around and I was fortunate enough to have her by my side. When I turned and kissed her, I could hear the final symphonic music begin that would signal the end of the movie and the rolling of the credits. It was a very happy ending and although I was sad to see the end, I looked forward to seeing a forthcoming sequel.

THE COMPLEXITIES OF COMPANIONSHIP

Like any other blind person, I don't always need a companion. When I am in familiar surroundings, I can exist quite happily by myself for relatively long periods of time. For example, when Nancy takes a trip without me, I can stay at my home for two to three weeks and do just fine. I cook my own meals, wash my own dishes, clean my own sink and do all of the things that a sighted person can do. Sometimes, I go on exploratory junkets around my property. I have learned that when I'm doing this, I should carry a cell phone and also setup some sort of aural lighthouse so that I can hear the direction of the location to which I need to return. I do this by playing a radio out a window. I might not be able to see the window, but I certainly can hear the radio from quite a distance away.

Indeed, there are times when I do better in the house than even Nancy does. This is particularly true when the power fails at night. Although the absence of light makes a tremendous difference to Nancy, it makes little difference to me. I enjoy the thrill of rushing up and down the stairs in a very quick manner as Nancy takes little baby steps to go from one room to another. In her power failure blindness she has asked, "How do you do this everyday, all day?" The truth is, of course, that I don't do this all day. I have developed over the years a virtual reality of what the house or my office or work place look like. Thus, I'm in a better position than she is since she has not spent time formulating this reality because it is unnecessary.

Nonetheless, there are times when a companion is really necessary for a blind person. Obviously, when I am going into new territory, I need a companion with me to orient me, to keep me safe, and to help me develop this virtual reality of the place where I happen to be. To the casual observer, being a companion to a blind person shouldn't be all that hard. What after all does the companion do? Grabbing on to a blind person and pulling that person along doesn't seem to be that big a deal. However, there are complexities in the relationship that need to be understood, and so using Nancy as my primary example, I will discuss right now some of those things that the companion to a blind person needs to consider.

First, there is a physical element to being a companion to a blind person. The first thing is how does one attach oneself to a blind person. I have found out over the years that the best thing to do is just to grab the elbow of the person guiding me. Over the years Nancy and I have developed quite a relationship here, and a soft holding and touching of the elbow is all that I require. I don't have to grab her in a death grip. I just need to know where the elbow is and how it's moving. Some people think that the elbow has to be extended to the blind person. When I first get a new connection with someone who wants to lead me along at work or at church or some other venue, the initial thing the woman I'm asking for help will do is to extend her elbow in an awkward horizontal position. It's as if the person who is helping me is getting ready for a major chicken dance competition at a wedding. This is all very unnecessary. Just letting the elbow stay where it normally would be is plenty of help. As Nancy or any other companion walks along, my attachment to the elbow will tell me which way we are going, how fast we are going, and whether or not I need to be aware of steps or movement down. The elbow, in fact, tells all. The one complication to this relatively simple truth occurs when there seems to be danger in the area because at those times I will grab on to Nancy's elbow a bit tighter. I also need to let her know when she is walking too fast for me because at that point I will start to drag her back by her elbow. While this movement might seem subtle for a few yards, over the course of a half-mile or so I can really put a lot of pressure on Nancy's physical structures. For this reason I often, on a long walk, stick a finger through one of Nancy's belt loops and let her pull me along that way, particularly if the terrain is relatively flat. We also have used something of a train method over long walks where Nancy grabs the front of my cane and I get behind her and put my hand at the bottom of the cane. As long as I know what hand she is using to hold the cane, I can get behind her and not worry about striking things at either side of us as we walk along. The horizontal cane keeps me focused on where Nancy is and helps me stay in position right behind her but not close enough to step on her heels. In addition to this physical element of companionship, there are also the psychological and emotional aspects. One of the things that is going to drive any blind person's companion crazy is the way people stare whenever they see something different or unusual. When Nancy and I enter a restaurant, some diners immediately stare and gape at us. These folks, in general, are easily distracted and have little going on in their own meager lives. When they see my cane, their jaws, I am told, immediately drop, allowing flies in the vicinity to land on their tongues. Now some people don't mind getting attention. I'm sure people with wild tattoos and extreme hairdos like Mohawks find it very pleasant to have people gawk at them. Nancy, however, is not such a person and it took her awhile to get used to the fact that people display such rude behaviors. Sometimes they even go beyond rudeness and poke each other to make sure that no one in their group misses the opportunity to stare at someone who is different.

The irony of all of this is that when Nancy and I are walking in public places and confronting oncoming pedestrian traffic, many times apparently they don't see us at all. I am six feet tall and weigh approximately 190 pounds. I am not a small object. I tend to carry my cane in front of me in my outside hand as I grasp Nancy's elbow with the other hand. Walking two abreast this way makes a fairly large and visible presence. My cane is a traditional one, white all the way up and down except for about five inches of red at the bottom. It is clearly a blind man's cane. Nonetheless, in the Woolworth's grocery store in Sydney, I was bumped into at least four or five times in the space of fifteen minutes by people who apparently had no idea what my cane was used for. This was not an isolated incident. As Nancy and I walked along an oceanfront path in the Sydney area, people who should have been able to see us 15 yards away would walk right up into us! With my hand on Nancy's elbow, there was no question that the physical connection was not a romantic embrace. My grasping of her arm seemed more like a child's than any other possibility, yet people just didn't seem to know what was going on.

Another thing that is hard for a sighted companion to get used to is how wide a distance there is from the right hand of a sighted person to the left hand of the blind person when the blind person is walking along on the left side of the sighted person. Occasionally, Nancy still underestimates how much room I actually am using to her right or to her left. She's pretty good about the distances but occasionally I nick something as I go by, especially when we are in stores. Some of my friends, who have limited experience in being my companion, get embarrassed when they walk me into something. I have a friend who has just started spending more time with me and provides rides to work. Janet is a very smart woman but in my first couple of trips to the school from the parking lot, she inevitably hung me up on the side view mirrors of automobiles--a very dangerous element of parking lot life for the blind. But Janet's case is not the worst. I remember a time early on in my visually-impaired life when a relative of mine walk me into a hotel column. The relative was quite embarrassed, and I was quite shocked to have made face-to-face contact with one of the support columns of this edifice.

Another unnoticed burden for Nancy is the huge sense of responsibility she feels as she assists me. She must anticipate every possible danger that might confront me in terms of changes of terrain that are unexpected. A one-inch lip or change in the height of a surface could cause me to fall--something that is going to look very, very painful to those around me. Sometimes the dangers come up very, very quickly indeed. On trains the gaps between the railroad car and the platform are often quite significant. In addition, the height of the rail car above the station platform can be quite challenging as one exits the train. In a recent trip to Spain, Nancy and I were getting off in the main station of Barcelona. There was a significant crowd trying to get on the train as I was getting off with a pack on my back. The people around me blocked Nancy's view of the gap that actually existed. As I stepped off the train, I stepped into nothingness. When I realized what was happening, I was quite shocked. Fortunately for me my movement forward and the weight of the pack on my back gave me enough momentum to tumble forward even though my left leg was thigh-high into the gap. When I hit the platform, my right leg curled underneath me and I did a small roll. This brought my leg out of gap but I was on my side on the platform. Nancy thought that I had surely broken my right leg, but I was all right! At the very same time that I tumbled, the crowd around me gasped. As soon as I realized I was safe, I then began to feel embarrassed that I had made such a spectacle of myself. I quickly jumped up to assure everyone that I was unhurt. Numerous people came over to assist me, but I smiled and shook my head again and again that I was all right.

Nancy felt terrible. She had taken all responsibility for what happened to me even though there was no way that she could have anticipated it on this day. As I said, the crowd blocked all view she had of what was happening on the platform. In addition, I was my usual anxious self getting off the train and perhaps sped out of our car a little bit too quickly. The noise of the people around me added to the sense of anxiety about making sure that I got off in a timely fashion. Nonetheless, even though I assured Nancy that it wasn't her fault, she kept blaming herself again and again for something she should have, in her opinion, anticipated. Nancy's reaction is just another example that sits on the shoulders of anyone who is assisting a blind person.

Beyond Nancy's guilt about the Barcelona fall, there is also a certain guilt she carries with regard to me not being able to see. She so wants me to see that it nags at her that I can't. As she was enjoying the spectacular sites in a place like Australia or New Zealand, she felt guilty that I couldn't see the things that she could. She wanted me to share her experience. I wanted to share these experiences too, but there was nothing I knew could be done at this point for me to see things she so enjoyed. While she had negative emotions about my not being able to see, I was enjoying very positive emotions about the fact that my planning and financial support made it possible for her to see the wonderful things that she was enjoying. I don't think that this paradoxical set of emotions is unique to Nancy and me. I believe that many people who assist the disabled find themselves worrying more about the disabled person than the disabled person does. Adding to the physical and emotional burdens that Nancy must bear as my companion, there is also a significant intellectual load that goes along with the job. Nancy is a very bright individual with a university vocabulary and a good background in architecture, art and nature. As a result, there is much that she observes about the places we visit. She feels a strong need to share with me the visual aspects of these experiences, yet if a picture is worth a thousand words, there are many, many words she has to form to describe the visual things that we encounter. Since traveling makes us encounter so many things, it is very difficult for her to edit what she wants to talk about and to provide the in-depth analysis and description she wants to give me for all of these experiences. It's as if Michelangelo had to paint a new masterpiece every four hours. No matter how much talent he had--and he had plenty--he just couldn't keep up a pace like this.

All of these pressures would seem to be plenty for a companion like Nancy. However, there is one more that is added to the picture. Not only do people like to gape and bump, but they also feel that they must talk and comment. They often make these comments close enough to us that we can hear what the people are saying. Nancy cannot believe how insensitive some people can be. Since she is very protective of me, she takes these insensitive comments to heart. The insensitivity usually isn't reflected in the negative things they say about me; rather they call attention to the fact that I have a disability and am different. Instead of letting me enjoy where I am, they put emphasis on the disability that I have. Instead of trying to get to know me as I fully am, they focus only on the small part of me that they see.

Because the job of companion is so demanding, I make sure that Nancy gets some time off for rest and relaxation away from her very stressful duties. In our trips I always make sure that every few days or so that there is an afternoon or even an entire day when she can go do those individual things that can provide her with some relaxation and happiness. In a trip to a museum or a shopping mall, she can indulge in those visual pleasures that are so important in those places. She richly deserves these opportunities. For my part, I can easily stay in a hotel room or travel trailer and find many things to do. Whether these things consists of making mental notes of experiences I have had in the previous couple of days or listening to university lectures on tape or hearing a good audio book, I have plenty to keep myself occupied. By employing this strategy, Nancy and I have been able to take trips that are of such length that even sighted people marvel how long we can keep pushing the travel experience. The 72 days we took on the Australia trip would not have been pleasant or possible if Nancy and I did not have this common ground for relaxation and recuperation.

REST-RUMINATIONS

One of my big disappointments from the Australian trip was that I did not get the answer to the question whether the water in the toilet circles around differently from the way it does up here in the States. Somehow I just didn't get around to it. I guess subconsciously I might have been put off by the fact that to make my study accurate, I would first have to reconfirm that the water in the toilet in Cortland actually flowed in a particular direction. To do this without letting Nancy know I was obsessed with such stupidity I would have to flush the toilet, put my hand in the water and assess its direction and then make a mental note about what direction the water was flowing. Once in Australia or New Zealand, I would then have to repeat the process there and make those ever so important mental notes. As the reader can see, I would have to be highly motivated to determine the answer to the question. I guess I wasn't that motivated.

Perhaps my aversion to the experiment was the lingering trauma I had suffered when rather magically my talking watch from Radio Shack had found its way into the toilet. I recall I was getting ready to go into the shower, I turned around swiftly to put myself into the shower and somehow--God only knows how—I hit the strap of my watch and raised it into the air and it flew without hitting the toilet seat or anything else, landing in the center of the toilet water. I was shocked when I heard the splash. I moved as quickly as I could, but it was all too late. Once I retrieved the watch, I had to figure out what to do. I knew from my sanitizing youth that I probably needed to wash it off, but I felt this was giving a drowning person a drink of water. Nonetheless, I gave it a quick wash and pushed all the buttons I could, trying to hear that wonderful sound of my talking watch. At first I heard a noise and my heart leapt! The female voice of the watch started listing all the hours of the day, but it wasn't a good sign. The hours went by faster and faster and soon they were hardly distinguishable from one another--then nothing but silence. I was crushed. I had the watch for nearly a year and it had served me well. Like a mature marriage partner, it was not the same watch I had purchased brand new but it was indeed a comfort partner in my experience of life. Its speaker element was dented; the paint had chipped off in some places; and the wristband was a bit tattered. Nonetheless up until her demise, the watch gave me timely and valuable information. I was sad to see her go.

From this experience you can see how bathrooms hold some special danger for me. In an earlier book I discussed my bathroom adventures along the Mediterranean coast, but my excursion to Down-Under was going to bring me new adventures despite the fact that I was in a region touted for its high technology and infrastructure excellence. One of the best parts of the bathrooms in New Zealand and Australia is that there are many handicapped bathrooms separate from the men's and ladies' rooms. These bathrooms for the disabled are not handicapped exclusive. While it seems to me that folks who don't have a disability should leave these bathrooms alone in the event that someone with a disability might come along, many fully-abled folks like to pop in. The reason is obvious. When one enters a handicap bathroom, it is almost like being at home because it's private. And certainly the individual who slips into the handicapped bathroom probably convinces himself or herself that the time will be very short and that no handicapped person could ever possibly need to use the bathroom at that time. I'd love to see the look on the faces when they open the door and see a person in a wheelchair waiting or someone like me standing there with his cane. Would the intruder in the restroom put on a dopey smile shaking his head a few times as if to say,"Oh hi, how are you? Yes this is a nice bathroom and it's waiting for you now. Here let me open the door for you." What a piece of chicanery and fraud this would be.

In any event I love to use these bathrooms because Nancy can give me a full depiction of the layout. I don't have to hunt for the toilet; I don't have to wonder if a urinal exists in the room. She lets me know where everything is, how the supplies look, and in fact if the room is ready to be used by a regular human being. A nonfunctioning toilet is one of the dreads that I have when I go into a restroom stall. I don't like to waste water but sometimes it is the best move to find out if indeed the toilet is operating properly.

Certainly one of the times one must use the restroom is before a long airplane flight. I try to avoid using the airliner's restroom at all cost or to minimize my visits, so the last minute stop in the airport restroom is very important. The Auckland airport is a modern facility with modern bathrooms. Not surprisingly, the airport has numerous restrooms for the disabled. Nancy and I located one of these near our boarding gate, and it seemed to be especially modern. However, I found when I closed the door that it had a strange quirk. Once the door closed a mechanical voice told me to press the button to secure the locking mechanism. Press the button? Where was the darn button? I put my hands where one might expect to find the lock on a door, but there was nothing of use there. I opened the door again and closed it again. Again the little voice told me to press the button to lock the door. I ran my hand around a number of different places, but I found nothing. I opened the door again and called Nancy for help. When she entered the restroom and we closed the door together, the voice again told us to press the button. Nancy looked around and indeed saw a red button way down near the floor over on the right side. She pressed the button, and sure enough the door locked! We then unlocked the door, and I let Nancy out. I could now be in the restroom with the door locked. Once again, the voice told me to press the button; this time I knew where it was.

Apparently this restroom was made by people who have a myopic view of who the disabled are. This seems to happen quite frequently, for many folks wheelchair accessibility is equivalent to accessibility for the disabled. Like everyone, the disabled community has a great deal of diversity that needs to be considered. Not only are there blind people like me, but there also people that have severe hearing problems and other kinds of issues that need some imagination and creativity to be applied if they are going to be able to navigate the complicated world of mobility that exists today. Another example may make this clear. When I travel alone --which is something I'm not terribly fond of--I often ask for assistance to get from one gate to the next. At the airports I'm told to wait at a particular place until someone arrives. Inevitably when assistance comes, I find myself in the presence of a young woman with a wheelchair. Now I can sit in the wheelchair, but I think it is silly for me to be in a wheelchair when I am very capable of walking for miles somewhere. I feel more comfortable just attaching myself to the young woman's elbow. But I guess the chair is what the folks above decided that any disabled person needs to use.

In Sydney I had the need to use the public restroom in the basement of the Victoria Building. Since the Victoria Building was nicely renovated and a tourist attraction, I felt that the restroom facilities would be quite adequate. Nancy and I noticed that handicap accessible bathroom was not available, so we went to the main men's room. Now Nancy and I have developed a strategy over the years where she will get as close as she can to being in the men's room to give me a heads-up about where facilities are. I can get a good start by at least knowing where the sinks might be and where a bank of toilet stalls might be. She has even gotten used to the fact that she can hear her voice echo against the walls of the men's room as she tells me to move more to the left or more to the right. I've almost gotten use to it myself. The problem with the Victoria restroom, however, is that it had been designed by the same people who built the set of Get Smart, a popular show in the sixties. As the reader might recall, agent Smart goes through many doors that automatically open and close. Such was the case in the Victoria restroom. As I took two steps past one door it slid closed. Nancy could not tell me where the sinks were because she couldn't see them. For a moment I stood in a no man's land between one door and another, but as I moved forward the other door opened. This was a new experience for me, but there were plenty of Aussies inside to assist me in finding the facilities I needed.

Such was not the case, however, when I visited a restroom in a café at Noosea Heads on the Queensland coast. After consuming several beers while Nancy was in the ocean swimming, I needed to make a restroom visit before we went back to our campground. A pleasant waiter pointed to the door that would lead to the restroom, and Nancy and I proceeded down a set of stairs. We then proceeded down another stairs--and another--and another. I soon expected the temperature to rise as we were clearly entering the bowels of the earth. After numerous descents and an uncountable number of twists and turns, Nancy saw a door that said "Men." I opened the door, and there was a little bit of corridor, then another door. Nancy did not follow me, and I said good-bye to her in the manner reminiscent of the way that Magellan said good-bye to his wife when he began his final and faithful sailing journey around the world. I was totally shocked at the setup of the restroom once I got inside. Everything was small in terms of the spaces available, and the room seemed to twist and turn with walls and panels setup all over the place. I could get no idea of the shape of the room at all except it was like a social services office in the Bronx. There had to be a hundred cubicles each offset by a direction that was not rectangular or predictable. When I finally found a stall I ducked inside. Upon exiting the stall, I faced a real problem. I had no idea where the door was! In addition, there was no one in the bathroom. There was no one to ask for directions. Nancy was not nearby. There wasn't an open entrance into the bathroom where her voice could carry. Indeed I wondered if she could hear me. I tried to find my way out several times, but I could find no corridor or walking path. Finally, after about five minutes of bumping into walls and sinks and urinals and doors to stalls, I just began calling "Nancy!" Eventually, I got a small kind of answer and proceeded in the direction of her voice. The whole experience was quite unnerving.

Indeed bathroom visitations for the blind are not for the faint of heart. In Alice Springs we stopped to change planes for our trip to Ayers Rock. We were in the Outback now, so when our plane landed in Alice Springs, I was not surprised that we had to walk down the stairs from the airplane onto the tarmac and then proceed to the terminal. It was about ninety degrees, and the terminal, although small, still seemed modern enough. One thing I did notice, however, was that the flies appeared to be an issue. As Nancy and I strolled to the terminal, a group of flies accompanied us into the interior. Whether the flies needed to make a connection or not, I don't know. I did know that Nancy and I would use the terminal for our usual restroom stop before our flight. When I entered the men's restroom, I wandered about for a while trying to find a urinal. None seemed to be present. I then noticed the sound of water and men proceeding near me to take care of their business. However, I couldn't figure out what the deal was. I did not sense anything that seemed like a trough which is the case in some men's rooms. I asked the fellow next to me what the deal was as I could feel some grate under my feet. He told me that where I was standing was a good enough place to do what I had to do. I said, "Am I facing the right direction?" He said, "Yes; just go ahead." I felt extremely uncomfortable as the reader can imagine. But, I followed his directions as much as I could. This was perhaps the strangest bathroom experience, because, to this day, I still cannot imagine what the setup really was. Also, standing on the drain that was part of the sewage system is not a memory I like to relish.

Besides the bathrooms in public places, the bathrooms in our rooms often produced a sense of wonder for me. Many times our agents had secured a room for the disabled for us because they had notified the various hotels that I was blind, and so the establishment would put me in a room for the disabled. This, of course, was not a room for the blind; it was for someone in a wheelchair. The good news was that often these rooms were a bit larger and gave me greater freedom of movement. It also seemed to make the clerks of the hotel happy that a disabled person was in the room for a disabled person. While there seemed to be no connection between the facilities and me, still a disabled person was in the room for the disabled! When properly designed, bathrooms for wheelchairs are huge. They have to be. However, the one thing that is tricky is the shower. Because the room is setup so that a person in a wheelchair can get into the shower without assistance, there is no lip or barrier to keep the water from the shower in the shower. What the builders do is to create a slope within the shower so that the water slopes down into the drain. When this is done correctly, it works pretty well. However, in a couple of the rooms I visited, the angle of the shower was not steep enough, and so the water in the shower inevitably streamed into the bathroom as a whole. This happened even if I turned the shower nozzle as much as I could to the wall and tried to be as careful as was humanly possible.

Sometimes I got into rooms that were what I call "almost rooms." They were almost handicapped accessible. What this usually meant was that a regular bathroom was retrofitted to become one that was fixed to help a person with some handicap, usually one of mobility. In one case in New Zealand, various handles and grips were attached to the walls to help a person with some physical difficulties to get up and down from the toilet. Unfortunately, the person who did the renovations never actually tried to use the toilet that had been renovated that way. The renovated hand-hold stuck out over the toilet so that it made it almost impossible to sit down. While my trip never caused me any injury, this was the closest I came to hurting my back, since I had to twist and turn to get my body located on the toilet seat in the proper way. In Waitomo, the place with the glowworm caves, a couple had spent a small fortune in renovating a cozy twenty-unit motel. Nancy and I could appreciate the cash that had gone into making this place comfortable for guests. However, we were both astonished at the shower that came with our room. Nancy and I had never experienced a shower of such force. We felt there was no variation in the amount of water or water pressure that would be produced. It was either off or at such a high degree of force that we felt our skins were being exfoliated. It is the only time in my life that I can remember I actually wanted to scream in the shower. I had to wash myself and clean myself but I didn't need to remove all three or four epidermal layers. If one of the things that skin treatments do to make the skin look young and fresh is to remove a layer of skin, then Nancy's skin and mine must have been among the freshest on the face of the earth. I also had never felt so clean.

The final area of restroom accommodations I wish to discuss would be those located along beaches. From my experience from when I was a boy in New Jersey, I never had expected much when I entered such a facility. In fact, I try never to enter such a facility. My sanitation nightmares tend to feature these beachfront locations. However, I was pleasantly surprised in Australia. While the accommodations were not luxurious, the facilities always seemed to be in working order and relatively clean. The plastic toilet seats that were in evidence seemed to be the norm, not only in the beachfront locations but even in the more expensive hotels.

I also did not find much evidence of vandalism. As a youth in New Jersey, I had often experienced restrooms where some of the facilities had been disabled or destroyed by someone. In a trip to Seville in Spain in 1986, I once went to some public restrooms where all of the facilities had been ripped off the wall as if I were at a construction site instead of a restroom. Of course, these facilities were unusable. I've often wondered about people who destroy bathroom facilities. I just can't understand them. As a human being, I know as I proceed around the world that

I need bathroom facilities. Everybody does. What does a person have to be thinking to destroy something that not only everybody else but he also needs to use? I guess the only people who would destroy any bathroom facilities are those who think that they no longer have a need for such devices. They must be contemplating suicide. In any event, I was pleasantly surprised at the beachfront facilities that I found in both Australia and New Zealand.

I hope these discussions of various bathrooms have not been troubling for my reader. While some would say that such topics should not be discussed at all, I think the availability of sanitary restroom facilities is an important part of travel. Indeed, for anyone who travels a long period of time, the nature and conditions of public restrooms is an important concern. For a blind person it is not only a concern, but also a challenge and, I must say, I have to cue up my courage quite a bit when I enter some of these places. Nonetheless, it is all part of the adventure.

2000 KILOMETERS TO BRISBANE

As Nancy and I put together our trip to Australia, we thought it would be a shame if we didn't use the sunny and mild climate of Australia to its fullest advantage. We thought that camping would be a great way to experience the natural beauty that Australia had to offer, particularly in the seashore rich state of Queensland. Furthermore, we convinced ourselves that camping would be a great way to meet the real citizens of this country. Nancy and I had camped often in America and had camped several times on our trips to Europe. We remember these experiences as among the best of the times we had in our travels. In addition, at the beginning of our discussions, we also thought that camping might be a less expensive way to see the country.

As our plans developed, a new element entered our considerations--my fear of snakes. While I knew I could avoid the box jellyfish by not entering the sea, I was not so sure that I would be able to avoid the poisonous snakes in Australia, particularly if I was visiting the campgrounds. Books on tape and my listening to nature programs on television had informed me that ten of the most toxic snakes in the world find their homes in Australia. Exactly where these snakes happen to be I wasn't exactly sure, but I knew if I ran into them I would sense them much too late. I could imagine myself getting up in the middle of the night in a campground and wandering to one of the camp restrooms. These are not very secure facilities, I imagined, and so it was not without question for me to consider that a coiled snake might be resting comfortably right next to the toilet bowl I was seeking. In a horror-movie way I imagined that such an encounter would be my last.

After discussing this scenario with Nancy several times, we decided that the best solution would be to rent an RV that contained a bathroom that could be used by me at night. As Nancy went through the options available to us, only one stood out. It was a 22-foot Mercedes-Benz motor home that included not only a kitchen and cooking facilities, but also a bath with a shower, toilet and a sink. This was not an inexpensive alternative, but from my point of view it certainly was a viable one. While the size of the motor home might intimidate some female drivers, Nancy had purchased a used motor home that was exactly 22 feet long in the year 2000 that she had driven for five years. Even though she would be driving on the other side of the road, I thought she could handle it and so did she.

Our plan was to take two weeks to drive from Cairns to Brisbane. It was a straight shot down the coast, and the two weeks we had allowed would permit us to spend a day or two at any campground we found particularly attractive. We located a grocery store just outside of Cairns that was part of a large shopping mall. We knew that this would be a great place to go to find convenient parking and to load up with groceries and supplies that we might need.

When we arrived at the RV rental site, Nancy and I were cautiously confident that everything would work out well. Our confidence, however, was going to slip a little bit within the next hour and a half getting acquainted with the behemoth we had rented. An older quite friendly Australian gentleman oriented us to the vehicle. Nancy and I were a bit shocked when he related to us the method of sewage disposal. Instead of the hoses we had become accustom to in the U.S., this vehicle had a removable cassette. It was something like a transparent plastic suitcase that received the waste from the bathroom above. When the camper needed to be emptied, someone from the RV would remove that "suitcase" from the vehicle and bring it to the restroom to dispose of its contents. Since we had never dealt with such an item, my imagination had difficulty seeing Nancy walking around the campground with our sewage in this transparent case.

Eventually, the clerk brought us to the driver's compartment. Nancy shuttered at what she saw. Instead of the automatic transmission she was used to on our motorhome, Nancy immediately saw that the transmission in this vehicle was manual. A very large and imposing stick shift stood up on the left side of the driver's seat. Not only was she going to drive on the opposite side of the road and read all the strange signs that would confront us, but she also was going to be manipulating the clutch with her feet and handling this large stick shift with her weaker arm. She was concerned.

After more instructions about the many dials that were in the driver's compartment, the agent bid us a fond farewell and we were ready to set off. We had to go down a very, very steep driveway, and within ten feet we knew something was wrong. A tremendous scraping and bumping rocked the rear end of the RV. Nancy hit the brakes, and we stalled with our front end a bit in the highway. She tried to restart the vehicle and get it going, but we had little luck. Finally, she jumped out and got the agent and he got us to the side of the road. When she asked about what was happening to the vehicle, the agent explained that the driveway was much too steep for the length of this vehicle and the backend was dragging along the driveway as it did every time someone left in a 22-footer. Nancy was simply incredulous. She then commented on the process of restarting the vehicle. The agent then said in order to restart, she had to do a special operation that meant revving the engine a couple of times while the clutch was fully depressed. He had not told us this, perhaps assuming that we had driven vehicles like this before. Somewhat nervous about this shaky start, Nancy got back in and restarted the vehicle. We began to move down the highway going from first gear to second to third and achieving sufficient speed to be in the flow of traffic. Eventually, we got into the fourth of the five forward gears that were available. There was no practice track, and Nancy had to figure out where the clutch engaged and where indeed she would have to place the stick shift to find the appropriate gears for travel. Although we hadn't gone a kilometer, we were beginning to feel as if things were moving in the right direction. All of a sudden we began to hear a steady beep from the dashboard. We wondered what it could be. Nancy noticed a letter appear on the screen in front of her but it had no meaning. We thought it might be a door that had been left ajar. We also thought that it might be something very insignificant. In Spain the previous year we had listened to a beep for about ten miles that turned out to be something to tell us that the radio needed to be reinstalled on the dashboard.

In a few seconds, however, we surmised that something serious might be going on. We began to smell something burning. Was it coming from a vehicle in front of us? As we continued, the smell got more and more intense. We both decided it was time to quickly pull over wherever we could. I had visions of the vehicle bursting into flames approximately two kilometers from the rental station! We quickly found the manual and paged through it trying to find some text that would explain the letter that Nancy had seen on the screen. Eventually she found the information she wanted. The letter was an indicator that the emergency brake was still engaged. Nancy told me that she had released the emergency brake, but when we worked it we found that it had not been totally disengaged. This particular brake had a point where it seemed to be off but needed to be pushed even further to get the total disengagement.

At this point both of our hearts were racing. Maybe this wasn't a good idea after all. Nancy began to suggest that maybe we needed to develop another plan. Perhaps a rental car and hotels would be the way to go. I told her that we were only a kilometer or two from the shopping mall and we could park the RV in the large parking lot and make plans from there. The smell of the overheating brake continued to be present in the driver's compartment, but we pressed on to that big parking lot. Once we arrived there Nancy and I grabbed the rental agreement and went for a cup of tea at a café that was in the mall. As we sat drinking our tea, I listened to Nancy vent her frustrations and concerns about the RV. I had seen her drive moving vans and back RVs into spaces where there were literally six inches on either side. However, the circumstances of this day really seemed to have gotten to her. We had invested several thousand dollars in the rental of the RV, and I wondered how much of this money we could get back. I asked Nancy to read the cancellation portion of our RV contract. As soon as she read the words that said that no credit would be given for any unused portion of rental time, I knew the die had been cast. Nancy knew it too, and I sensed a new determination in her. Within ninety minutes we had purchased groceries and were driving out of Cairns and down the coast. As each minute passed I sensed Nancy's determination morphing into execution, so by the time we neared our first nightly stop, we had driven about 100 kilometers, and Nancy was beginning to show confidence.

We had been driving in and out of torrential downpours for about an hour and fifteen minutes when we arrived at a crossroads called El

Arish. There was a small motel at the roadside that also had a number of campsites available. With darkness coming on, Nancy pulled on the gravel driveway. She said that she would sign us in and I waited in the RV. After about ten minutes Nancy came back. The office had been locked, but as Nancy walked around she found an open door. On a table in clear view of this open door was a purse and soon the mistress of the establishment appeared. She apologized for being in the shower and explained that the office was locked because she was concerned about security. When Nancy and she both looked at the purse that was in clear view of the open door, Nancy told me that both she and the owner had a laugh.

This was not a place that was going to get a separate page in a campground magazine. I quickly named it the Bates Motel and Campground. Not only was the owner strange, there were only two or three other vehicles in the campground. These folks were not transients like us. These were people who had made their travel trailers into their homes, and as my son would say, there was something very "sketchy" about the whole thing. However, since it kept raining pretty heavily and darkness had come on, I was not too worried about people roaming about and getting very close to us. In addition, our RV was so well built that it seemed to me to be more like a fortress than a camping accommodation. As the rains beat down on the roof of our roaming home, I quickly went to sleep. Not only did the vehicle give me a sense of security, but also Nancy's driving had shown me the confidence that my travels the next day would be in safety and not in terror.

The next day might be called the day of 180 degrees, for the changes that took place within 12 hours were quite remarkable. First, the weather had improved and as we drove south, the torrential rains ceased. Secondly, it was clear that Nancy was in command of the vehicle. The third change had to do with our next campground that we found in a place called Ayr. While the Bates Campground had shown some neglect in the care of the grounds, the next campground seemed to be cared for by a rather anal German. Every site was clean and well positioned; every blade of grass was manicured; every building was in perfect repair. In fact, things were so much in order that I nicknamed this campground the Adolf and Eva's Campground. Indeed the construction of the bathrooms reminded me of the Third Reich, for the walls were so thick that it seemed to be built to last a thousand years. However, we only stayed for one night and as the next day arose we took our chances on where our next overnight location would be.

If change is at the heart of the nature of things, then our next night at Eight Point Beach and Tourist Park was in the left ventricle. This campground was in a place called Serena, a hub of coal mining and transport activity. As a matter of fact, one of the longest docks in Australia had been built in this area for the transport of coal to various parts of the British Empire. As Nancy read me these facts, I had some misgiving about the scenic and coastal beauty of such a place. Arriving at the campground, then, was not as surprising as it might have been. The tourist park itself appeared to be something from a B-Hollywood movie. A restaurant, bar, and campground reception office were located in a large wooden building that had clearly seen its better days. It reminded me of the large type of wooden mansion that might be part of a western town that Clint Eastwood might have dominated in his spaghetti western days. Everything, including the people, was a bit rough around the edges. On the positive side, there were plenty of available campsites. Frankly, the place was nearly deserted. As we drove to our site, we got quite a surprise. The owner of the tourist park had purchased a series of metal containers that might be placed on large, ocean-going containerships for the transport of goods. He had converted these into one-room accommodations for those who did not have an RV. The containers, of course, were metal and were equipped with an air conditioner. There were, however, no tenants at this time. As we drove to our site, we saw only one sign of habitation. A series of gray uniform shirts hung from a single clothes line. I wondered what kind of person would stay at such a place like this. When Nancy told me about the color of the shirts, I asked if a serial number had been printed on the pocket. The place seemed the perfect setting to encounter a man who escaped from prison, had just been released from prison, or was on his way to being returned into prison. Although I enjoy the lack of crowds in my off-season traveling, I do sometimes find it unnerving to be the only campers in a place or the only campers with the exception of another person who might be indeed a bit "sketchy."

Before nightfall a woman with a couple of children made her way into the campground. This group had apparently been staying there for quite some time, and their presence gave me some comfort. However, as we prepared for bed that night, I made sure that the RV was totally secure. Although I slept with both eyes closed, one ear remained open the entire evening.

With few regrets, we left Serena the next morning and made our way to Yeppoon and the Beachside Caravan Park. In our alternating pattern of our accommodations, this campground was reminiscent of Adolf and Eva's place. It was neat and well cared for, and with its beautiful location it was nearly full. As we checked in, Nancy pointed out to me an emergency medical box on the outside of the main office. This box had materials and instructions for what to do if someone was stung by a box jellyfish. Such a safety device clearly reminded me that going in the water was serious business.

The sea surrounded the campground, and the bay around us was always full of tidal activity. When the tide was out, it was several hundred yards to the water's edge. When the tide was at its full, the waves would break just below the perimeter of the campground. I particularly enjoyed high tide in the late evening and at night. The breaking of the waves provided a wonderful masking noise that made all other disturbing sounds disappear. I think I can make up a little motto for how this helps me to sleep overnight. It might go like this: "High tide at ten; my sleep will begin." The other important factor about the tide is that it had an effect on how we proceeded to the village of Yappoon. Most of the time Nancy and I could take a beach walk and arrive at the center of town in this way. It was only at the full of high tide that the ramp going to the center of town would be covered by water. Since this only occurred about an hour and a half a day, the high water didn't cause us much inconvenience. Walking along the beach provided us with an opportunity to see marine activity that was of interest. Various kinds of small crabs dotted the shoreline. Some were green, some were blue; some were solitary individuals, and others piled on top of each other like ants in a mosh pit.

It was at this campground that we made our first serious connection with some native Australians. At the site next to us were a retired couple named Barry and Lynette. They were gracious and warm individuals who had visited the United States several times. Barry had been a mining engineer, and they had traveled across the entire width of the

United States. We chatted everyday before we left and they treated us to a steak dinner at their campsite.

The friendliness of Barry and Lynette and the beauty of the Beachside Caravan Park had made our camping experience there one of those that we might have wished to extend for a few more days; however, it was still a long way to Brisbane, and we needed to get there by a certain date. So we set off again to continue our travels on what is called the Capricorn Coast. The coast has been given this name because at Rockhampton, a city on the coast, the Tropic of Capricorn passes right through the center of town. The imaginary line that is the Tropic of Capricorn serves as a bookend to the Tropic of Cancer which circles the earth north of the equator as the Tropic of Capricorn circles the earth south of the equator. What is of great importance to note about the Tropic of Capricorn and the city of Rockhampton is that this line marks the southern boundary for the natural occurrence of salt-water crocodiles. If one looks at a map of Australia and marks the Tropic of Capricorn from east to west, every body of water either fresh or salt that is north of that line might be a habitat for a salt-water crocodile. Weighing up to 2000 pounds and as long as twenty feet, these creatures, oddly enough, can be very difficult to see in the water. They spend a good deal of time totally submerged. As they glide along in the water, special projections in the skin on their backs make it possible for them to move without much of a wake or a ripple at all. In short bursts they can literally spring from the water with the propulsive movement of their great tails and snatch an unsuspecting human being or other creature from the shore in just a second. Like the great white sharks of the ocean, the salt-water crocodile is a magnificent eating machine. Those in the know say that all people approaching a body of water north of the Tropic of Capricorn should stay away from the edges and not enter the water unless they had been assured from someone who knows the area that there are no salt-water crocodiles in the water.

As we drove down the highway, Nancy and I mused about the wide range that the salt-water crocodile had. It was good to muse. The highway from Cairns to Brisbane was flat, straight, and noisy. Most of the time there was only one lane in each direction. To keep costs down, the builders of the highway had not used the highest grade of asphalt. A pebbly, grainy surface is the rule on almost one hundred percent of this road. As a result, tire noise is quite high. Only in very rare instances is a smooth patch of asphalt encountered where the noise reduction is clearly audible.

As Nancy drove along now, the terror of earlier days had disappeared. Now the enemy had become complacency and fatigue. I tried to find music that might keep her interested, and I inserted the few CD recordings we had to keep her entertained. I asked her about the scenery, but there was not much variety. Occasionally there were some interesting trees, but most of the land was filled with sugar cane. In addition, because Australia is so unpopulated, there was not much of man-made building and civilization to provide a distraction. As a result, when there was something to stop for, we stopped.

We were heading for a place called Lake Monduran, but before we got there, we began to see signs for a roadside stop called Calliope. The sign said that there was a small restaurant there as well as a small historic village. Nancy loves the latter, so we pulled in.

We had been out of the rains for a while now, and Calliope was showing the effects of the drought we heard about so much during the earlier parts of our trip. The dam that fed this area had dried up, and the restrooms in the rest area had been converted to composting toilets. Dryness had brought a sense of withering to everything. In the restaurant, the horn of plenty had withered, emptied and dried; there were no more meat pies! Even the women in the restaurant had an air of desiccation. They were an older bunch, and as I listened to their conversation, there was no moisture or vitality. As they talked, it seemed that their lives and possibilities had all dried up. I was saddened by this, but I was also struck by the strange coherence of aridity that seemed to consume the entire place.

When Nancy returned we set off again, but we were quickly looking for another diversion from the boring highway. In her <u>Lonely Planet</u> guidebook Nancy had read to me about a place that served mud crab sandwiches. It was getting close to lunch, and my mouth moistened as I recalled the wonderful mud crab lunch I had on the Catch-A-Crab boat. The place where we could find this crab luncheon was Miriam Vale, so we pointed ourselves in that direction. Unfortunately, the guidebook did not indicate the name of the restaurant that had the mud crab sandwiches. We asked in one restaurant and than another.

We went down a side alley and into a small delicatessen that might have this reward of the day. As we entered, I felt the person behind the deli case brighten; however, when I asked for the mud crab, he told me he had none. I then asked if he could tell me where I might be able to find these sandwiches. Sadly but competently, he told me that the sandwiches were sold at the convenient store at the end of the street. As we left, I could feel his disappointment. We were perhaps his last hope to move that piece of ham or bologna that could last only one more day in his case. We did eventually find the sandwiches, but they were a disappointment. They did not have the flavor that the mud crab had on the boat. I drowned my disappointment not in a beverage but in a kangaroo burger that had some taste. As Nancy and I left this eating establishment, we heard a call for help. A man had apparently locked himself in a restroom that was accessible from the street. Nancy went over and chatted with him to discover his problem, and he claimed that he couldn't get out. I could only think that it was some sort of scam, but Nancy decided to help this pathetic individual and went back into the restaurant for help. Astonishingly, the fellow had actually locked himself in the bathroom and needed a person from the restaurant with a key to help him out. Feeling like the ultimate rescuers, Nancy and I shook our heads at each other and headed back toward the RV.

At about two hours before sunset we arrive at Lake Monduran. One of the things that was attractive about it to us was that it was off the main road, so there wouldn't be traffic noise disturbing us. The campground was populated by two groups of people. One was a caravan club from an adjoining town; the other was a group of fishermen that had come to Lake Monduran for a weekend fishing derby. Of course this surprised me since the country was in the midst of such a great drought. When one of the competitors in the fishing derby came over to assist us in getting hooked up to our utilities, I asked him about the state of the lake. He told me that the lake was down considerably from when it was full but it was still fishable. He pointed out that although fish were in a small volume of water, they were now protected by much of the debris that is normally not part of the fishing experience. The boats have to deal with the many branches from falling trees that were now very much in play as the boats went about their fishing.

The next day we moved on to Hervey's Bay where we would spend three nights at the Pialba Campground. Hervey's Bay is a tourist center for fishing trips as well as for detours for excursions to Frazier Island, the largest sand island in the world. We selected a site right on the beach, and because we were in the off-season there was plenty of room all around. We did however get some neighbors when a delightful family consisting of Troy and Stacey and their two children Riley and Mason moved in near us. Troy and Stacey were friendly Australians, and their son Riley was a studious young man about eleven years old. Mason, the two year old, was as cute as they come but also was in a state of constant locomotion. He immediately fell in love with our RV and spent every moment he could sweeping with a little broom around and under our motor home as well as taking every chance he could in trying to get into the RV. I enjoyed his presence but had to be somewhat careful in the event I would slam the sliding metal door of the RV on his small arm or hand.

While Frazier Island and a fishing trip were top items on the agenda for Nancy and me originally, another place served to be one of my favorite memories of this trip. On our first full day in Hervey's Bay, we had gone for a walk looking for a café for lunch. We found a café in a nearby mall, but workers were painting the hallway outside the café, and the smell of paint was incredibly thick in the air. We decided to find another place to eat and asked one of the locals where we should go. She mentioned a couple of places and she then said, "Of course, the RSL is right over there." Nancy and I had no idea what an RSL was, but we went to investigate. Nancy and I found a large building that had a large parking lot around it. As we walked in we found out that this was a Returning Servicemen's League Chapter. The best way to describe it would be for me to say that it reminded me of a VFW that had been constructed on a Las Vegas scale. When we entered, I vaguely remembered that these places not only provided a service for members but also provided services for outsiders who signed in for the day and became temporary members. Inside the club there were bars, restaurants, and gambling. In addition, the prices appeared to be forty percent lower than they were at other restaurants and bars.

When we went upstairs and ordered our lunch, I was stunned at the value I was getting. Both Nancy and I had extremely large platters of food that contained not only the usual vegetables and carbohydrates but also significant portions of meat. I ordered wine with my meal, and Nancy also had a beverage. My pleasure was unbounded when I added the total bill and found out that we had spent about $14 for a lunch that could certainly hold us until dinner and even until the next day if necessary. With the friendly attitude of the people and the pleasant surroundings to boot, I became a RSL member for as long as I was going to be in Australia!

Our evenings at the Pialba Campground were quiet. Being near the sea, the waves provided a masking sound for any other noise that might be in the vicinity. On one night, however, the tide had gone out quite far; I awakened at about quarter to eleven and heard some sounds in the distance--louder than what I usually heard. I was surprised to hear anything in the campground at this time since in Australia campgrounds generally have a rule for quiet hours starting at ten and going on until seven. I was shocked to hear any noise at all. The people making the noise were not young people because there were no young people except Riley and Mason in the campground. These were people who clearly were over fifty-five who had been long-term residents in this particular campground. As I listened for a few minutes more, all of a sudden I heard an authoritative voice telling the individuals they would cease the noise they were making or they would be leaving the campground immediately. From that point all noise ceased. That was the exact kind of action and result I so often longed for in American campgrounds, particularly the state campgrounds. I know such order is difficult to achieve, but when it happened in my presence at Hervey's Bay, I felt just wonderful.

Our next move was to a high-end resort area called Noosaville. This is the suffix capital of the world. The Noosa region of the Sunshine Coast has a cache similar to Princeton, New Jersey. Because of its association with quality, many businesses use Princeton as an address for their activities. Similarly, because of its association with the homes of millionaires and affluent visitors, many communities want to have Noosa in their names. As a result, there is a Noosa Junction, Noosa Head, Noosaville and as many other combinations that one can put together that begin with the prefix Noosa.

Part of the reason for this specialness is the topography and geographic location of this region. A fresh water river flows a good distance from a national park right down to the seacoast. The seacoast provides an entrance to the ocean that is protected at the end by Frazier Island and one has the ability to enter a protected bay area or go out into the ocean as one chooses. In addition, the topography has some rolling hills with some nice foliage, and another national park sits on the seacoast for a fine variety of recreational choices. We were fortunate to be able to see this area because the municipality has a campground right on the river. The municipality leases the campground to a private management company who keeps the campground in top shape and takes care of all the hospitality.

When we arrived at the campground, we did not have a reservation and so we had to settle for at least our first night on a site that did not have electricity. The sites in this unpowered area were quite close together, but we were glad to have a place to park for the night. About a half hour after we had set ourselves up, a small van size RV parked close to us. I'm not thrilled with people so close to me, but sometimes the nature of the experience forces me to accept this when it happens. What really got to me, however, was that as soon as this young camper finished setting himself up he began to play music. Up until his arrival nearly 200 campers had not found it necessary to play any music at all. What possesses someone to start playing music when none is in the air is beyond me. At first, the music was rather loud. It was not heavy metal, but I think only someone with a great deal of arrogance or ignorance could believe that he could play music that would satisfy all the tastes of the campground. In addition, there were many birds in the area of very beautiful hues and, of course, sounds of their own. Wouldn't it be better for people at a campground by a river to be listening to the sounds of nature and the songs of birds? Perhaps a thought like this came to our neighboring camper or at least part way, for after about half an hour he lowered his music to about half. After another half hour, he discontinued the music altogether. Oddly enough, once his music stopped, two young females in their early twenties who were camping on the other side of us began playing their music. It was something of a young people's relay team I would imagine. Their music unfortunately was not as pleasant as the first person's music. However, this music also ended in about an hour. It was now about 9 p.m., and quiet had settled on the campground.

All the various population points of Noosa are close to the river. To make transportation between these points as easy as possible, a ferry runs between the population points on the river, and passengers can get on or off wherever they wish throughout the day. On our first full day camping here, we went on the ferry and had a wonderful lunch at a restaurant up river. One of the things I will never forget about my ferry ride back is the captain of the small ferryboat. He was a man in his forties who enjoyed talking to the passengers as he made his runs over and over again. We learned much about this individual from his commentaries. Apparently, he was in his second marriage and had two children in this second marriage. In addition, he also seemed to have developed great regrets about his choices in life. This became apparent when he began describing to us the various properties that were in prime locations along the river. He would talk about one house costing $2 million; he would then point out another house that might cost $4 million, and then he would discuss the great amount of money that it took to acquire this island or that island or to make substantial renovations to the property before us. He was very envious of the monies that were spent. I have never been a worshipper of celebrities, and I know I never will. As a result I never oohed and aahed over the kinds of things that money can buy. I have met wonderful people who had a lot of money, and I have met wonderful people that have little money. It seems to me that money is not the determinate of personal quality. Consequently, I found the ferry pilot to become quite annoying after awhile. We were trapped on his boat; if he needed to vent his frustrations about his life and his envy of the rich, he should have gone to see a therapist.

When we were eventually able to get off the ferry at Noosa Head, I was quite glad to get away from the carping about cash to enjoy one of the real gems of the Sunshine Coast. In a country as big as Australia, Noosa Head really shows off what can be special in a relatively small place. The beach at Noosa Head is relatively small, but it is sandy and it is flanked by some rocky outcroppings. The surf here is active and entertaining. As soon as Nancy saw it, she decided that she wanted to take a dip. Before she headed for the breakers, however, she deposited me in a small outdoor café very close to the sea. Although I could not wet my body, I could wet my whistle. I listened to the crashing waves and imagined Nancy cavorting in them as I consumed a few very pleasant Victoria Bitter ales that were offered at a fairly reasonable price.

The next day we headed for The Palms Campgrounds at Maroochydore. On the way we stopped at a pleasant little place called Maryborough which happened to be the home of P.L. Travers. Travers is the author of the popular children's book <u>Mary Poppins</u>. At one of the bus stops along the main street there was a statue of Ms. Poppins, but I was disappointed because it was only about two-thirds life size. It seems to me if you are making a statue and you already invested two-thirds of the material, why not come up with the rest and make a very imposing statue indeed? On the other hand, Maryborough was doing lots of great things. In our short stay, we saw a revitalization of numerous historic streets and the renovation of buildings that had important connections to the history of Maryborough. I believe that in a thousand years Australia is going to be one of the great historical locations in the world. It is indeed a relatively young country right now. Captain Cook's adventures here in his ship, the HMS Endeavor, took place around 1770. The roots of Australia's independence date from the 1850's. However, every location I had visited in Australia had historic monuments, buildings and districts. Having been to cultures that have existed for thousands of years, I often find the designations of historicity somewhat premature. I am a bit used to this because in the area where I live buildings prominently display the fact that they have been around for less than two hundred years. There are even some businesses in my home area that proclaim quite proudly that they have been in business for seventeen years! I guess I have a longer sweep of history than two decades. In any event, the one positive thing that such a premature passion for history will accomplish will be that these buildings and areas will be preserved for posterity. This is especially important if the buildings happen to be made of wood. Furthermore, modern builders don't seem to compete very well with the Egyptians, Greeks, and Romans in terms of the longevity of their structures. It was therefore, not surprising that Maryborough had a strong sense of its own history. Although it was not touted much in guide books, Nancy and I found Maryborough relatively rich in restored and preserved buildings and streets that seemed so important to those with a penchant for history. In fact, there seemed much more preserved here than in other locations that receive much more attention in the guide books we were using.

From Maryborough we once again set out for our final destination, Brisbane. Nancy's driving had become a matter of course by this point. Parking on city streets and parking lots had become routine. On the highway the trip had become even tiresome at times. All the terror was gone except for those moments when we encountered a roundabout. Taking a traffic circle when all the usual traffic patterns had been reversed is indeed an exciting motoring moment. The hardest thing to do is to look in the correct direction for oncoming traffic. This, of course, is true even when one is a pedestrian. Numerous tourists have been killed crossing streets because they looked the wrong way for oncoming traffic. In London busy intersections often have words painted on the sidewalk and on the streets telling pedestrians to look right as they step off of the curb. Besides this concern Nancy also had to consider the size of the vehicle and, of course, our destination. Since many of the names have aboriginal backgrounds, they are not easy to remember or to recognize. In some cases the new words are often fairly similar to other names of towns and villages. As I indicated earlier, Brisbane as a destination point of reference was usually not prominently displayed as a traffic direction in the circle. With few exceptions, Nancy handled these moments of excitement with her usual aplomb. When we arrived at The Palms, we knew we were getting close to a major population area because this campground was wonderfully constructed. It was large with many sites, and it had a wonderful swimming pool with a spa attached. The landscaping was impeccable, and the facilities were very well maintained. One of the features of Australian campgrounds is that barbeques are often included in a central area. In addition to the barbeques, which are operated by electricity or gas, campgrounds provide numerous tables in the area as well as sinks for the washing of dishes. Quite often groups come together to cook their evening meal and sit at one of the tables nearby. Unlike campgrounds in other countries, the tables and the barbeques are not spread out over a large area. The idea is for people to come together and converse. To address the quality of this campground, I vividly recall on one of the days we were there a family had planned a reunion weekend at the campground.

It was quite remarkable to see a family of 25 people or so using the center cooking area as one might use a banquet facility.

From Maroochydore Nancy and I took several day trips. On one day we decided to visit the Big Pineapple. Like the lobster and the rocking horse we had previously visited, the Pineapple was indeed very big. It was part of a farm that produced many tropical delicacies including, of course, pineapple. The restaurant inside the pineapple took advantage of all the fresh produce that was available. In addition to the restaurant, the farm also had a small wildlife refuge that customers would reach by getting on a small train that would take them down the hill to the wildlife park. The usual suspects were all in attendance: koalas, kangaroos, dingoes, exotic birds, etc. Nancy found particular joy in a mule that had a pleasant and engaging personality and, incidentally, tried to kiss her.

Many times during the trip Nancy would want to exam the products that were available in the gift shop. I needed something to do as she viewed what was for sale, and this usually meant that I would have a cup of coffee. While Nancy examined the offerings of the Big Pineapple, I sipped a cup of coffee near the entrance to the small train. As it always seemed to happen, I didn't have to wait long for a woman to begin talking to me. Today, the woman's name was Diana. I don't know if she saw my cane or not, but she walked right up to my table and began chatting with me as if perhaps we had gone to school together. I usually enjoy this instant familiarity, and I listened intensely as she began to provide some of her personal history. She told me that she was from Perth and sometimes it got hot in Perth. The next thing I knew she was telling me that she enjoyed sleeping in the nude. If I missed the point that she enjoyed sleeping in the nude when it was hot, she brought this point to my attention several times. Now we had only known each other for a few minutes at most. I have a very good imagination. I was somewhat affected by these repeated reminders of her sleeping habits. I'm sure if I could have seen myself sitting at the table, I would have noticed that my skin color had taken on a hue similar to many of the tropical flowers that decorated the Big Pineapple. I can't remember a time in my life when the conversation went from an introduction to intimacy so quickly. Therefore, I was quite relieved when Nancy returned and we set off for our next destination.

The next day we set out for The Australian Zoo. The name of the place suggests that this is a public zoological garden, but this is not the case. This is a private commercial venture owned by the Irwin family. The principle member of this family was Steve Irwin. Steve, the crocodile hunter, was well known because of his television productions and more recently because he had been killed by a stingray. Despite his death, the zoo continues to function as a vibrant commercial enterprise. To entice tourists to come to the zoological park, the Zoo sends motor coaches to various towns and cities within a reasonable driving distance. These coaches are free, so Nancy and I availed ourselves of this opportunity to visit a wildlife park that had a fairly strong reputation. The double-decker coach that greeted us was quite impressive. Once we began our trip, the driver put on a video of the life of Steve Irwin. The driver also had numerous video copies of some of Steve's shows. The picture of Steve that was presented in these biographical videos was amazingly positive--perhaps too much so for my cynical mind. During the course of the presentation, the narrator pointed out that Steve's mother used to rescue creatures that had been injured. One of the creatures she rescued and brought back to health was a stingray. When I heard this, the spirit of Greek tragedy peered over my shoulder. Could this have been the very stingray that caused Steve's death?

At the zoo we paid our entrance fee and entered. The admission charge was over thirty dollars apiece. In addition, there was no concession. In Australia, the word "concession" is used to describe a discount that is often given to the disabled. In order to get a "concession," one must ask for this discount at the ticket booth. Sometimes the "concession" is quite significant. At one wildlife park that Nancy and I had entered, she was admitted free of charge because she was assisting me. In order to not insult me, the agent charged me nearly full price. At other places there would be a discount of twenty or twenty-five percent. It all depended on the place.

Once inside, the high admission price did indeed include some value. The place was Disney-like. By this I mean that the buildings were modern and well designed and all the walkways and landscaping were of the highest quality. There were also plenty of animals and many exhibits. Of course there were elephants and tigers, crocodiles and kangaroos. There were also animals that I didn't expect to find. A

Komodo dragon, for example, was on exhibit. This is certainly one of the nastiest creations God ever made, but it was somehow exciting to be near one. We also spent sometime watching one of the attendants feeding a Tasmanian Devil.

But the big deal was the big show in the amphitheatre. It's here where things got a bit out of hand. It was one thing for us to have Steve Irwin speaking to the audience on a big jumbo-tron screen; it was quite another for a character in the show to come on stage with a gigantic Steve Irwin papier mache head on and take part in the show's presentation. Then after Steve had been brought back to our attention, his wife and children did various presentations on the jumbo-tron. Of course, there were animal activities also presented on stage, but the insistent and incessant presence of Steve was overwhelming. On our way home on the motor coach, we went over the top. The driver played more and more of the Irwin videos. It just got to be too much. Before this trip I would have wondered if any nation could out do the United States idolatry of the Kennedy Family. I think I had found my answer at the Australian Zoo because the Irwins here had risen to an even higher place in Australian idolatry.

With this experience behind us, we spent the next day driving to Brisbane and ending our trip of 2000 kilometers. Like our first pick up station, the rental depot outside of Brisbane featured a very steep driveway. This time the driveway rose steeply up from the rental station rather than down. When Nancy and I finally dropped off the keys and all the paperwork was signed, we nearly jumped into the air with excitement about the fact that we had brought the motor home back, after 2000 kilometers, without any major incidents. We did have a cracked windshield, but this had occurred because of a random rock that had been thrown up as we traveled along the highway. Fortunately, we had purchased overall coverage for the vehicle, so we had to bear no further expense for the repair of the windshield. We had had many wonderful adventures in this two-week odyssey and had met some really wonderful people. Nancy again had astounded me with the grit she can bring to bear in certain circumstances. In spite of the stress that this portion of the trip placed on us, Nancy and I both agreed that these two weeks were some of the best that we spent in the two months we had in New Zealand and Australia.

DIONYSIUS DEFEND US!

When I was an undergraduate in college, my alcoholic beverage of choice was beer. Of course, I was not alone in this because beer was relatively inexpensive. In fact, because my friends and I were much more interested in price than quality, we often got some wonderful bargains. One that I remember particularly well was a sale that was held by one of the local supermarkets for a product called Topper beer. Topper was selling at the time in a special sale for $2.00 a case! Even during the mid-sixties, this was an incredible price. Beer was not allowed in the dorm, but my friends could not resist such a marvelous sale. What they did to get the case of beer in the dorm was rather infantile but also rather effective. They would dress up as if they were going home for the day or the weekend, and take a suitcase with them. The suitcase, of course, was empty, but it looked the part and was big enough to contain a full case of Topper. There were three hundred young men in the dormitory, so there was a lot of coming and going. As a result, it was easy for a student to leave the dorm at 3:00 p.m. pretending he was going home and to return again at 3:35 p.m. after having a refreshing day at his family home. Once the Topper got into the dorm, it was placed in a desk drawer, which had been lined with aluminum and plastic and contained a good amount of ice.

Such were the beginnings of my engagement with beer. This continued when I went to graduate school. However, after I had reached the age of 21, the carbohydrates in beer began to catch up. Specifically, my weight increased from a rather attractive 170 pounds to a somewhat unattractive 230 pounds. Beer and potatoes were the cause. When I looked for an alternative alcoholic beverage, wine became the clear choice. It contained no carbohydrates, was consumable at a slow pace for a relatively long time, and--most important of all--it could be cheap. For example, when I was pursuing my doctorate at Syracuse

University, I regularly bought a gallon of Skytop brand burgundy that cost $4.99. Although this wine had a bit of a bite, it still was a tremendous bargain.

Some might object that although wine has no carbohydrates, it does contain calories. They are in fact correct. All I would have to do is think of Sergeant Garcia from the Zorro television series to realize that wine, in fact, can be part of a fattening diet plan. Sergeant Garcia, a man who was almost spherical, was depicted in the television series drinking wine in large amounts on a fairly regular basis. I also remember him consuming large quantities of chicken. In moderation a wine and chicken diet plan might work. In the amounts that Sergeant Garcia consumed, a super model would quickly become obese.

Thus, as I formed a life plan in the early 1970's, wine had become an important part of my beverage foundation. I was lucky too. The consumption of wine in the United States began to take off in the '60's and continued to increase spectacularly after that. For some reason, perhaps the connection with the sophistication that some Americans equated with European cosmopolitanism, wine became fashionable.

Unlike soccer, which would still take decades to catch on in America, wine caught on pretty fast. As a result, the bite that was part of my Skytop experience actually began to disappear. To be sure, there was still some bite around if one wanted to look for it, and I often did. I knew that the bite would be the bargain. When I visited Spain for a semester in 1986, buying cheap wine was always on my agenda. It was not Rioja region wine; it was from the bit-of-a-bite region.

However, as the wine craze continued and increased all over the world, quality got better and better even at the lowest prices. It became possible to buy wine that had no bite--even at fairly low prices. I was able to leave off the drinking of burgundy, a rather uninspiring experience and was able to begin to consume my dry red favorite Cabernet Sauvignon.

Obviously, there are various grades of Cabernet Sauvignon. The bite was gone, but there are still subtleties of flavor, smell, and appearance. However, most of these differences mean little to me. The way I look at it is this. There is a tremendous difference between a car that sells for $10,000 and a car that sells for $70,000. In other words, the Yugo and Mercedes are quite different. The difference, however, between a car that costs $30,000 and one that costs $50,000 is often not worth the difference of $20,000 in price, at least in my opinion. I would always choose a Cabernet that costs $4 as opposed to one that costs $20 because, to be frank, the fact that one has a slightly different color and slightly more rich walnut taste is not worth $16 to me.

It is clear then that I have a love of wine-- inexpensive wine. Most of the time, I can find an inexpensive wine that I can drink at my home or in my hotel room. However, at the beginning of my trip to Australia I thought that this basic pleasure of mine was not going to be available, even in a country that is producing more and more wine each year not only for domestic consumption but for export around the world. When Nancy and I arrived at Sydney, I wanted to bring a bottle of wine back to our hotel room. We stopped at a bottle shop near our hotel where a rather snooty young woman in her early thirties told me that I couldn't buy a 750 ml. bottle for less than $10. In a country that produces as much wine as Australia I found this price incredible. I did not buy the wine at the shop but committed myself to finding wine at much less than $10. After walking a few blocks, I purchased a bottle for $7. I felt my beliefs about the price of wine had been validated, but I was not satisfied. I began to hunt for something even cheaper. Of course, the place I found the holy grail of wine was the land of cardboard. Although I think that the cell phone is one of the worst inventions of the twentieth century, I strongly believe that the cardboard box of wine where the wine is encased in a plastic bladder is one of the greatest inventions of the millennium. Once I got over the idea of being embarrassed by asking for boxes of wine, things began to happen. I found that the Australians were indeed technologically sophisticated. They had two-liter boxes of wine, three-liter boxes of wine and four-liter boxes of wine! These boxes were at very attractive prices. The best I was able to do for a four-liter box of dry, red wine was $7.20 (U.S.). To put this in perspective the snooty woman's bottle of wine would have cost $8 (U.S.) for three-quarters of a liter. I was now drinking wine that cost $1.80 for a full liter! The bonus was that there was no bite at all!

Nonetheless, if the world of wine was heavenly in my residence, it was almost hellish in the world of restaurants. Like the United States, New Zealand and numerous other countries around the world,

Australia is part of an international conspiracy that seeks to violate rules of hospitality even more than the Cyclops Polyphemus did in Homer's Odyssey. In that epic Odysseus seeks to obtain hospitality during his wanderings. When he and his men stop at the cave of Polythemus, the Cyclops does not offer hospitality but begins to eat them! A similar kind of outrage occurs in a restaurant when five ounces of the cheapest red wine available winds up costing a customer like me about $5.00. I have ordered the cheapest wine that the restaurant has to serve. It tastes exactly like the wine I get out of the cardboard box. However, instead of spending 5.5 cents per ounce as I did when I bought cardboard wine in Australia, the bill for the five-ounce glass of wine is $5, or $1 per ounce. People complain about the cost of furniture that is sold at five times the cost of production. The wine in the restaurant that I am talking about is eighteen times what I pay for it at retail. The production cost is even less than the 5.5 cents per ounce. To me, this seems like incredible gouging, and it is taking place in a restaurant where hospitality should be the rule of the day. However, I must point out that some countries that are sophisticated and civilized do respect this notion of hospitality. Italy is such a country. I remember on numerous occasions sitting down for a meal in Italy and getting a carafe of wine that was less expensive than a carafe of bottled water at the same restaurant. In fact, wine was half the price of canned or bottled soda.

Fortunately, there are still a few places in Australia where I could get a fair deal. One such place was the Ozone Hotel on Kangaroo Island. Nancy and I spent a few days here, and we were lucky enough to stay at the hotel on Schnitzel Night. This was a big night in town. The restaurant served beef schnitzel, pork schnitzel, and chicken schnitzel. In addition, the hotel also had a nightly happy hour. This happy hour, strange to say, was only an hour. But the values were fantastic. I selected a "cask" wine. I assume that "cask" was a restaurant euphemism for wine that came from a cardboard box. In U.S. currency the cost of this glass of wine was 88 cents. This is still about three times per ounce the price that I would pay in retail, but I thought it was fair. In addition, the Ozone Hotel presented a glass that was nearly to the top. It was not a gigantic glass, but it was big enough. I really get disgusted by places that provide you with a gigantic glass that they fill up from a third to a half. I guess restaurants do this so we can swirl the wine around and smell it. As a blind person, I'm not swirling anything.

I must confess at this point that I have a masochistic streak. This is revealed in the area of wine whenever I agree to go on a wine tour of some vineyard and participate in some tastings. Nancy and I have taken our adult children and various friends traveling down the Finger Lakes Wine Trail in central New York, and so it was not surprising that we visited the Barossa Valley Wine Trail near Adelaide. A wine tasting usually consists of a small--very small--amount of six wines. The amount of wine given per glass is so small that it can only be measured in atoms, not ounces. Even though I have attended tasting several times, I'm still shocked by the incredibly small amount of liquid that is in the glass. I usually hurry to put the wine in my mouth because I'm afraid it's going to evaporate by the time I get a chance to taste it. Part of the process also includes a lecture on the pedigree of the grape, the characteristics of the taste, and also the smell that I should be experiencing with the sample that has been presented. I guess the wine sellers have to tell me what the wine should taste like because there are so few atoms that my taste buds couldn't tell what is in the glass in front of me. To make this charade complete, saltine or oyster crackers are provided so that I can remove the taste from my tongue before I go to the next glass of wine.

In most cases the tastings are free or require a very small fee of a dollar or so. However, the low price isn't the result of generosity. The tastings are a hook. What the vineyard hopes will occur is that I will feel an obligation to purchase a bottle or a case of the wine that I had tasted, partially because of the nature of the atmosphere and partially because I feel that somehow I have a connection with the vineyard as a result of the sample tastings. The psychological marketers are right that I should buy something for the hospitality that has been offered-- as small as it is. However, when I find out the cost of a bottle of wine, I usually can resist the urge to buy. How can it be that the bottle I am looking at can cost the same or even less at a retail store than it does at the vineyard! There is no retail markup that needs to be considered. There is no transportation from the vineyard to the liquor store that needs to be added on to the cost. Yet, whenever I go on one of these wine tours, I feel I'm in the presence of another rip off--just like the rip offs that take place in the restaurants. Oh how I wish that Dionysius would come down and throw a scare into these grasping and greedy grape growers!

Another aspect of wine touring is eating lunch during the tour. Many vineyards have a restaurant to serve patrons who are visiting their establishments. When Nancy and I were in the Barossa Valley, we took advantage of such a luncheon opportunity. As happens in many up-scale places, the atmosphere of the restaurant was quite nice. It was in the cellar of a building that had been decorated quite handsomely. While prices for the food were not cheap, they were not as expensive as the various bottles of wine. What caught our attention here was not the food, but the attitude of our waitress. At home, in Central New York, the training of the wait staff is abysmal. I guess I can make this clear by pointing out the phrase that usually gets under my skin quite quickly. The words that offend so deeply are "you guys." Frankly I am shocked that a waitress would address Nancy and me as "you guys." This phrase is so informal and establishes a level of intimacy with the waitress that I have no interest in pursuing. Nancy and I often wonder how we have become friends so quickly with the waitress. Yet, this is just a symptom of the sloppy informality that often occurs in restaurants in Central New York. In the Barossa Valley we got to see the other side of the equation. While the waitress had apparently been trained, the training had gone beyond the usual to brainwashing. The phrase that this waitress used was "It is my pleasure." No matter what happened or occurred, the waitress would predictably respond, "It is my pleasure." We could have told the waitress that her nose was running, excessively big hairs were growing out of her nostrils, and she was the ugliest woman we had ever met, and she would have said, "It is my pleasure." While I found this somewhat amusing, Nancy got very irritated. I guess this is because Nancy is very egalitarian whereas I don't mind a bit of hierarchy now and then. In fact, I'd like to see more hierarchy in the world that I live in. For example, I believe in hierarchy of talents. I don't believe that everybody who can speak should be doing TV and radio commercials. The current rage to have man-on-the-street types giving their opinions about everything when they can hardly think or talk is frankly as annoying to me as the phrase "It is my pleasure" was annoying to Nancy.

In short, the hospitality industry--even in Australia--has a lot to do to prevent the revenge of Dionysius. A reasonable glass of wine at a reasonable price is a good place to start. Otherwise, owners of restaurants had better start wondering if Dionysius has contacted Zeus for the rental of a few hundred bolts of lightning.

THE PAIN OF TRAINS

As far as I can remember, I've always had a love affair with trains. Maybe part of this was the Lionel train set our family had when I was a boy. Maybe it was the fact that when I was a freshman in high school, I journeyed from Bayonne, New Jersey, to Manhattan and took the Jersey Central Railroad as my means of transportation to New York Harbor. I was fascinated by the steam locomotives that still appeared as well as by the shiny silver Budd cars that employed a diesel engine. These motorized Budd cars belched a dark exhaust smoke that today would seem extremely polluting. However, compared to the coal-fired locomotives that would thrust volcanic columns of black smoke from their cinder-spouting throats, the Budd car was a distinct improvement. The train was also very dependable in a way few things in my teenage life could be. When I arrived in the terminal and saw twelve trains waiting to depart at various times, I knew that when the hour and minute came for departure the train would leave. The Raritan Clocker was announced to leave at 4:14 P.M; at exactly 4:14 P.M. the long train would begin to slide smoothly and dependably out of the station.

I also had a very positive attitude toward the New York City subway. Although graffiti vandals would disfigure the outside of the cars, I always felt a wonderful satisfaction with these underground magic carpets. One could travel amazing distances in such a short space of time it seemed to me. And the cost--well, the cost was very small, in my opinion, for the ability to move so quickly in a crowded city. Furthermore, the subway cars during the early sixties were filled with some of the prettiest women I had ever seen. Secretaries from all over the city were still taking the subways in their short skirts and high heels. They completely transfixed me, and my appreciation of female beauty surely developed most fully as I rode through the urban caverns of Manhattan.

As I got older, my fascination of trains continued. In Europe I took trains in England, Switzerland, France and Spain. Each experience was exhilarating. I felt as if I were indeed living the life of a fictional hero. When Nancy and I took the overnight Talgo from Paris to Madrid, I had the sensation that I was a leading character in a James Bond movie. So, when the opportunity presented itself to take trains in Australia, I could hardly contain myself with such a prospect. Furthermore, taking a train was one thing; taking an overnight train was even better. On the overnight train one could not only go from destination to destination but also do so in such an efficient manner. As I slept, I would be actually accomplishing something in moving from one city to another. It was all so exciting; it was something I just had to do and something that I longed to do.

As Nancy and I approached our train in the Sydney terminal, I was excited, as one would be getting ready to meet an old friend. However, as we approached our railroad carriage, my excitement became somewhat muted as the sound of the engine and the powerfulness of its roar engulfed me. I have never liked being around large machinery that produces a kind of roaring sound. Not only does the sound cut off my sense of the environment I happen to be in, the size and hardness of the great machine makes me fear that if I make a wrong move something terrible might happen. I have often found this with construction equipment that I might be walking by in one of my journeys. Usually at this point I get up really close to whatever companion is near me. If I am alone tapping with my stick, I very often just stop and wait for someone to come over and assist me. The whole thing is very unnerving.

However, of course, Nancy was at my side and when she saw me reduce my walking speed to one that would enable a garden slug to pass me with ease, she grabbed my arm and guided me into the railroad carriage that contained our sleeping compartment.

Our compartment was great. Although it was small, it was modern, and when we closed the door, we were in our own little world. Sydney, Australia, is a great city, but it has millions of people. Closing the door to the compartment gave us a space that was all our own, and I relished it tremendously. After doing her usual survey of the appointments in the compartment, Nancy gave me the tour. Most important was the bathroom that would serve our compartment and the one right next to us. The sink and toilet in the restroom slid into the wall! The engineering was such that any water, either from the toilet or the sink, would cascade within the wall and not get into the restroom. What a piece of engineering! The key for me in my tour was to imagine how I would escape from my sleeping compartment and get into the restroom without locking myself out of the sleeping compartment. On the other hand, I had to consider how I would properly lock myself within the restroom. Door handles and locks needed to be located and memorized. Once this was accomplished, Nancy and I sat back to await the movement of the train, a good dinner meal, and--best of all--a good night's sleep.

As the train began to move, we heard for the first time an announcement over the loudspeaker that served our compartment. Apparently, it was important that no one miss any announcement because the volume level of the speaker was incredibly high. Nancy looked for volume controls and shut off switches in vain. Whenever the speaker spoke, we would have to listen. While this was an obvious safety feature, it was also a tremendous annoyance feature. Every announcement on the train blared its way into our consciousness.

The most annoying of all the announcements had to do with the food service. Now, I love food, and I usually like to talk and think about food. However, every five or ten minutes an announcement would come on telling us what foods were available in the dining car and at the buffet counter. This would be followed by another announcement telling us how much time was left to order and pick up such food. Another announcement would follow to tell us about the status of cleanup and the restocking of shelves in the buffet area! This was all too much information for me. The sad fact is that such information continued right up through the evening. At ten-thirty at night I'm really not interested in hearing that in twenty more minutes the buffet will be closed for fifteen minutes while the crew does some restocking in that area. I just can't imagine what a restaurant would be like that kept opening and closing its doors to customers so that some members of the staff could get something done—work that could get done without closing.

As a result of all of this incessant commotion, Nancy and I did not really settle into to our beds until about 11 P.M. I say that Nancy and I "settled" into our beds, but this is perhaps an overstatement. As we were lying down with Nancy in the top bunk and me in the bottom, we began to feel the motion of the train that we hadn't experienced sitting up. One of the first things I noticed was that the connections between tracks were not very smooth. In fact, at times I thought we were actually falling down a step as the train moved along. In addition, the train moved and swayed along all points of the compass. At times, I would feel the train pushing me in the direction of my feet, and my feet would hit a wall and take all the weight of my body. Then, all of a sudden, I would be tossed in the direction of my right arm. Bracing myself, I would then feel a surge toward my left arm and would have to brace myself in that direction. At other times the train would push me up toward my head, and I could feel my neck muscles bearing all the weight of the G-forces that were coming my way. I guess if the train had been moving more quickly, the G-forces would have be even harder to withstand. However, the train rarely moved above forty miles an hour. Track maintenance was certainly an issue!

If my plight on the lower bunk kept me awake, Nancy's plight on the upper bunk must have been shear terror. At times she was tossed into the air and I could hear her landing back on her mattress in the bed above me. Also, since she was higher up, the G-forces at work seemed to be moving her body more than mine. Of course, she is shorter than I am so she faced much more movement towards her feet and her head in the bunk above me. It was odd that we didn't spend a lot of time communicating with each other at this point. It was obviously apparent to both of us that neither one of us could sleep, yet we had no conversation about the roughness of the ride and the fact that at 1:00 A.M. both of us were still wide-awake. I guess, as experienced travelers, we knew that we were in a situation that no one could make any better.

It is also true, of course, that if we contacted the staff of the train in some way, they would not really understand our problem. The staff of the train acted as if the train we were on was the most spectacular, most efficient, most well run, and most luxury train that ever existed! Even when we were awakened at 5:30 A.M. with the announcement that breakfast would shortly be forthcoming, the conductor who entered our compartment had the air of someone who was awaking a couple who had been sleeping like babies for ten hours. I almost felt that if we had asked the conductor about why every compartment had to listen to those darn announcements all night, he would have responded, "What announcements?" I had seen this kind of service response many years before in the waiters of the restaurants along the beach of Torremolinos, Spain. On days in January and February when the temperatures might be somewhat cooler—fifty to sixty degrees-- the waiters would stand in front of open-air restaurants with towels on their arms as if the temperature was eighty degrees. As Nancy, the children and I would approach these restaurants in our parkas because of the wind and cool sea air, the waiters would present an image totally different from the reality that we were experiencing. The trainmen on the overnight from Sydney to Melbourne acted just like this.

When Nancy and I arrived in Melbourne, we were a bit tired. However, compared to the passengers who had not had compartments, we were quite fresh. We had had three hours of sleep; they had had little or none. Furthermore, we had had about twelve hours of privacy away from the masses. For me this psychological rest of twelve hours away from human interaction was well worth the cost of the compartment.

Because of this rather disappointing train trip, Nancy and I discussed whether we wanted to cancel our train trip from Brisbane to Sydney at the end of our stay. We thought about whether or not a rental car would serve our purpose better, and we also thought about what would happen to the monies we had put into the train reservation and how that would all work out. We concluded that we would give the railroad a second try many weeks later at the end of our stay. "How could it be any worse?" we asked. At the beginning of May we would get an answer to that question.

I think that one always can tell that a train trip is not going to be what one hoped it would be when the first thing that is done at the train station is that the passengers are herded onto a bus. Buses are different from trains. We were told that we were going to take a three-hour bus ride from Brisbane to a town named Casino on the Queensland and New South Wales border. The need for this bus service resulted from the fact that the train did not go fast enough to make the round trip from Brisbane to Sydney and back in the scheduled time.

Consequently, some time had to be saved by putting us on a bus and meeting the train along its route back to Brisbane. I can just imagine making arrangements on the Queen Elizabeth II and finding out that I would be joining the QEII somewhere at sea after I had been deposited on a cargo ship that would meet the QEII for its turnaround voyage.

Adding to the fun here was the fact that the bus wasn't in tip-top shape. The air conditioning unit had some problems with its condenser and fan. In fact, this air conditioning unit was the loudest I had ever heard. Up to this point I had only heard such loud noises from refrigeration units in grocery stores with wooden floors that seemed to be in the process of going out of business. Yet these were super quiet compared to the AC unit that Nancy and I encountered on the bus. The good news was that the air conditioner masked most of the conversations around us, so we were not victimized by people who had a tendency to speak too long and too loudly. However, there was one character in the front of the bus whose voice was capable of overcoming even this aural obstacle.

By the time we arrived at Casino it was dark. With about one kilometer to go, the road around us seemed very lonely and dark. However, we soon passed a McDonald's restaurant, and the driver announced that we could go to that McDonald's if we wanted to get some food for the rest of our journey. Unfortunately, the bus driver did not stop at the McDonald's, and he proceeded at least another kilometer to the train station. Who in his right mind would take a one-kilometer trip in the dark to McDonald's to come back again to the train station when the train was expected within twenty or twenty-five minutes! As we waited in the train station, I noticed that no one in our group had a McDonald's bag. All of us, however, were living in a fool's paradise. If we thought that the train was going to be on time, we certainly were carrying the thoughts of unbridled optimists. Pretty soon, we heard an announcement that the train was running about twenty-five minutes late. This announcement was repeated for the next forty-five minutes or so. Obviously, if one had taken seriously the first telling of this mechanical announcement, the train was going to be much more than twenty-five minutes late. Following this rather strange announcement and its sense of time, another announcement reached our ears. By now the reader of this book can see that on the

Australian railroad, announcements are a very important part of the service that is provided. The second announcement indicated that when the train arrived, there would have to be some cleaning and restocking done. The speaker of the announcement assured us that such activity would take no more than ten minutes. As the British might say, this was pure rubbish. The train is today the poor cousin of the airlines. We all know that on the airlines, pilots are trained to tell us that things will take place in much shorter periods of time than anyone with a sense of reality would think possible. The phrase "short delay" can mean anything from several hours to several days! The train personnel have learned this lesson well.

Fortunately, it was a nice evening, and so Nancy and I wandered outside to observe what was going on out there. Toward the end of the platform a young man strummed a guitar, and the competence he displayed produced some lovely music. Unfortunately, this lovely music was interrupted by a woman using the most terrible piece of technology ever invented--the cell phone. She spoke in a voice that wanted to proclaim her words and concerns all over the railroad platform. She indeed could be an announcer for the railroad who did not need a loudspeaker. Not only did she speak loudly on one call but she then decided to do all her business for the week while she was waiting for the train. As people passed her, they would look at her indicating that she was making a spectacle of herself. As Nancy and I passed her we too looked at her indicating that she was making a spectacle of herself and was indeed being quite obnoxious and annoying. As is usual with the cell phone user, these social cues have little effect. There has been considerable evidence that cell phones placed near the head can have some negative impact on the brain. I think that cell phone usage destroys that part of the brain which regulates social consciousness. After excessive cell phone use, people finally lose all social consciousness and speak loudly and publicly on matters that only one's intimates either want or need to hear. Because we wanted to escape from the volume of this woman, Nancy and I walked down to the other end of the platform, where we passed by another engrossing human drama. A young woman was clearly violating the space of a male whom, it was clear to us, she was trying to pick up. As we listened to her conversation, however, we could see that her chances of establishing a romantic relationship with this gentleman were getting slimmer and slimmer. She informed him that her various substance abuse problems were coming under more and more control. From her behavior it was clear to us that they were not under control although they might be, as she said, getting closer to control. In any event the next time we saw the gentlemen, he had freed himself from any connection with this female, and she spent her time refocusing her attentions on an unfortunate conductor.

When the train finally left the station, we were already about an hour late. As Nancy and I settled into our compartment, I mused about the name of this train service. It was called XPT. I quickly concluded that XPT stood for Extremely Poor Transportation. However, Nancy and I are nothing if not optimists, and as we put on our sleeping clothes, we mused about getting a few hours of good sleep. The train ran on the same type of under-maintained tracks that we had experienced to Melbourne. In this case, though, the connections between the tracks were a slight bit smoother. What this course from Casino to Sydney offered was a roller coaster kind of roll and sway that had not been as prevalent in the Sydney to Melbourne run. I was reminded of the little kiddy roller coaster I rode when I was a child at Uncle Miltie's Amusement Park on First Street in Bayonne. Now we would go around to the right of some geological formation and then around to the left and the car would sway a good deal to the right and then a good deal to the left. The turning made the train go quite slowly--approximately thirty to thirty-five miles an hour during the trip. I was on the top bunk this time and never went airborne. The swaying, however, did have a certain rock-a-bye effect. And Nancy and I both got twice as much sleep on this particular run as we did on the previous one.

One thing that was the same was the constant annoyance of the announcements. We were again awakened at 5:30 A.M. with the same train staff who were smiling as if they had again operated on the most efficient and wonderful vehicle ever created by the hand of man. Bleary-eyed, Nancy and I drank our beverages and ate our breakfast sandwiches. Nancy noticed a few kangaroos and sheep out the window, and this perked her up considerably. When the train finally pulled into the Sydney station, we were in good enough shape to face the world and with the help of one of the conductors made our way to the cabstand.

These two train experiences remind me of the BB King song

Daniel J. Pukstas

"The Thrill Is Gone." I had spent two nights with the object of my romance--the train. A romantic night can sometimes make or break a relationship. Clearly, for me, the bloom was off the rose. Yet as I record these thoughts several months after the event, I can sense in my heart a longing--a longing to once again hit the rails. Certainly, I will be willing to take another chance on a train in Europe. After sufficient time to process what I experienced in Australia, I might even take another tumble on a train in this great country—perhaps a train in the Outback. Amtrak, however, is a relationship I'm still not sure I can risk my heart on.

RISKY BUSINESS

There is no other way to say it--New Zealand and Australia are risky places to live. The two islands of New Zealand sit like gigantic potato pancakes at the top of churning and bubbling oil that threatens to eventually fry them to a crisp. Volcanoes, of course, are common on both of the major islands of New Zealand. In Auckland, there are 48 volcanic cones within the city limits! Some of these are extinct; some are dormant, and some are ready to blow. In fact, the danger of volcanic eruption is so much on the minds of the citizens of Auckland that in the Auckland Museum there is a large exhibit devoted to what could happen if the volcano erupted in the city. Actually, this isn't an accurate representation of the exhibit because the exhibit is not devoted to what might happen; it is devoted to what <u>will</u> happen. It's a wonderfully done exhibit, and school children who visit it just love it. It's fun to listen to them shriek and scream as they stand in a model house that trembles on its base while fires and explosions burst outside the windows of this structure. These spectacular special effects are there not to introduce children to what has happened in the past but to prepare them for what will inevitably happen in the future. The city of Rotorua also speaks with volcanic voices. Geysers, steam vents, and all sorts of bubbling earthly caldrons are part of the everyday in Rotorua. In addition, the city suffers from halitosis--a particularly severe case of halitosis that is highly sulphorous in nature. Magnificently scenic lakes exist in the craters of dormant volcanoes called <u>calderas</u> but the question that is on everyone's mind is: "When will the waters in those lakes be turned into steam as a result of the next eruption?"

Nancy and I were fascinated as we walked through the main public park in Rotorua. Police tape had been strung up in many places to set off open steam vents that had popped open through the soil. Some of the places that had exhibited volcanic activity through to the surface were in the children's playground! Within jumping distance to monkey bars a steam vent had opened up.

If volcanic fire does not singe one's heartstrings, New Zealand can also provide a water scare. The islands are touted as water playgrounds, and the sailboat is king of the sea. However, the waters, although breathtakingly beautiful, are loaded with sharks. Even on our way from the airport to our hotel, Nancy and I were introduced to sharks. As we crossed a small inlet in our shuttle van, the driver pointed out that the inlet was densely populated with sharks, although he noted that these were only eight-footers. With so much of Auckland's activity centered on the water, those dangerous dorsals add an interesting tingle to whatever the day's activity might be.

As any visitor to Down-Under learns relatively quickly, the Kiwis and the Aussies are intense rivals. This competition is one of the greatest in the world. In the area of fear, concern, and risk the Aussies don't have to take a backseat to New Zealand; there is plenty to worry about in Australia. For instance, the continent of Australia is ravaged by great cyclones in the period from February through April. Furthermore, the northern and eastern coastlines of Australia are prime targets for tsunamis that spring from earthquakes that develop all over the Pacific Rim. In addition, massive brushfires, like incendiary title waves, ravage vast areas of land and threaten even the great cities such as Sydney. If this were not enough, great droughts suck the life out of the continent. These droughts are not the exaggerated or made-up droughts that are developed by the Weather Channel in the United States; these are real droughts. The Weather Channel can declare a drought in a city in the United States that has already received 24 inches of rain in a year. However, what these hucksters then do is to tell the audience that in a certain period of time this city—that has already received over two feet of rain—is still several inches short of its average rainfall and is, therefore, in some state of drought. But 24 inches of rain is plenty in the big scheme of things! In Australia, on the other hand, things are much more severe. When Nancy and I visited Brisbane the city was down to 11% of its total water capacity. Some towns in the suburbs had already lost their entire water supply. This was not a matter of not washing one's car or not watering one's lawn; this was a matter of survival. This was the real deal.

But mega natural disaster risks are not the only thing to worry about in Australia. In my case I was much more worried about personal risks. I was very conscious of the box jellyfish. I had heard about this amazing creature many times, and I knew that its sting was not only life threatening but incredibly painful. As a blind swimmer, I had always considered jellyfish and sharks among the greatest concerns I had when I was in the water. The stonefish was another sea attraction that I hoped to avoid. This sea devil burrows under the sand in relatively shallow water. It has large, highly poisonous spines that can inject a toxin into one's foot and can do unbelievable damage. While my research has shown me that the purpose of these spines is still somewhat unclear, their insertion into the foot of an unsuspecting swimmer can cause pain that redefines the term human suffering. In fact, the pain has been described as so intense that people have sought to commit suicide just to allow them to escape from this hellish nightmare.

Sharks, of course, are a highly publicized element of Australian aquatic fun. On a short fishing trip in Harvey's Bay, the boat I was on and another which was fifty yards away caught several sharks. The next day Nancy asked me if I wanted to go for walk in Harvey's Bay, the very body of water in which the sharks had been caught. She noticed after a little while, with the water up to our knees, that I became reluctant to take anymore steps. She asked me what was wrong. I really didn't feel comfortable being in the same water where I knew sharks would be swimming. She asked me if sharks would venture into water that was only knee deep. I told her about some of the news stories I had heard about bull sharks off the coast of Florida that attacked children who were playing in water that was knee deep. Once I gave her this information, we laid out a course for the two of us to reach the nearest beach.

If the presence of sharks isn't enough to get the adrenalin flowing, then the salt-water crocodile can be counted on to get the adrenalin flowing in buckets. Ranging up to twenty feet in length and weighing up to a ton, this world-class killing machine can also be as quick as a cobra. With a split second striking range of up to ten feet, this perfection of perdition can snatch an unsuspecting individual on the shoreline in the blink of an eye. In the water the crocodile can out swim even the best Olympic champion. If these creatures were only found in a few salt-water basins that were in isolated parts of Australia, this would be bad enough. However, they are much more wide spread and can be found in any fresh or salt water north of the Tropic of Capricorn. Thus, the place where a salt-water crocodile might be lurking includes any body of water that exists in about one-third of Australia.

I often give good advice; sometimes I take it. On the issue of the salt-water crocodile I had numerous discussions with Nancy before our trip that under no circumstances would I go in a body of water that might contain a salt-water crocodile. However, when I got an opportunity to go on a boat to catch mud crabs, I threw my advice over the side. I had been afraid in a tour boat someone might shout out that a large crocodile was on the opposite shore and that the whole boatload of people would clammer to one side and capsize the boat. Once in the water, we would become lunch. Yet, the lure of crabbing was too much. Armed with the advice of many Australians that possibly—no, probably—I would be safe, I decided to take the chance. I really enjoy that word "probably." Like those who are willing to take the risk of a volcano or tsunami I was prepared to take the risk of meeting a gargantuan man-eating reptile. When I told Nancy of my decision to go on this crabbing boat in these crocodile-inhabited waters despite all of the conversations we had had on the subject, I'm sure she thought of the bumper sticker that said: "All men are idiots, and my husband is their king."

If all of this were not enough, I have also read many times about the toxic snakes that are native to Australia and the other threat to humans--the funnel spider. These creatures concerned me even more than the box jellyfish and the salt-water crocodile. Obviously, if I wanted to avoid the jellyfish and crocodile, I just needed to stay away from the water. The snakes and the spiders were another story. I wasn't exactly sure where the snakes would be found, but I had heard that the spiders could be found in hotels and motels. Fortunately for me, I never ran into a snake while I was in Australia, and the funnel spider never provided me with any room service.

Although the tourist might have concerns about the risks that are present Down-Under, the Kiwis and the Aussies take it all in stride. In fact, the Kiwis often like to add risk to their lives. For example, mountain climbing and rock climbing are important sports in New

Zealand. Furthermore, there always seems to be some sort of extreme activity that one can join. In Auckland, bungee jumping is quite popular. The city's central tower features bungee jumping for several hours during the day, as do other high buildings in the central business district. As Nancy and I sat in our hotel room at 7:00 P.M., the darkness of the night was shattered by some blood curdling screams. It wasn't a mugging that was taking place on the streets; it was bungee jumping taking place outside our hotel window. Additionally, in both New Zealand and Australia surfing is a major recreation. Like a miniature Spanish Armada, hundreds of surfers can be seen bobbing and paddling on the waves heading towards the beaches outside Sydney. The sharks that we hear so much about have no chance of routing this armada. In addition to those who love to take chances in the air and on the sea, many Australians head to the northern part of the country to sample the northern jungles and to enjoy the flora and fauna that are part of this exotic landscape. The fact that snakes and crocodiles also inhabit this special region seems to be a risk that many find worth taking.

In the commercial world there also seems to be a fascination with this risky business. In Waitomo, people have waged their economic and financial futures on fly larvae that live in caves. The special attribute of these fly larvae is that they glow. These so called "glow worms" (arachnocumpa luminosa) have formed the basis for the establishment of hotels, restaurants, and transportation companies. Not much else has economic viability in this region. Interestingly enough, the larvae state for this particular fly lasts for nine months. When the fly evolves out of this state, he lives as an adult for only four days. During the four-day adulthood, the fly procreates and then dies. As I learned about this fly, I began to think about life in the United States. With our Nanny State in full operation, the possibility of becoming an adult is being pushed further and further away from people. Some people have not yet achieved adulthood even when they are at retirement age.

How risky it is to place all of one's assets on the back of a fly? One virus, one special kind of bacteria, or one unforeseen predator can destroy the economic foundation of an entire region. This is certainly risky business in its purest form.

Similarly, Phillip Island makes a living on the little fairy penguins that live there. These penguins--about a foot tall--come ashore each evening and go to their nests. The number of penguins is not all that large--approximately four hundred. Yet, over the decades the sight of watching these penguins come ashore in groups and then walk to their nests has become a public fascination, if not an obsession. Thousands of people, perhaps four or five to each penguin come and sit in grandstands around the beach. The beach has floodlights on it, and as the sun goes down, the penguins begin to come ashore. People watch the penguins in their small groups as they come ashore, check for safety, and then go to their little nests. Rangers, restaurants, waiters, hotels, and all sorts of tours are banking on this nightly return to home to make incredible amounts of money. The total weight of the penguins is small, about a ton for the entire group, but these very animals produce an annual economic return that must be in the millions of dollars.

In truth, the hysteria about the penguins is quite unbelievable. Tourists from all over the world jostle each other--rudely in some cases--in order to get a better viewing position. Although warned by rangers not to use cameras, a clicking sound like massed machine gun fire can be heard anyway. As a blind person, I was given special attention by one of the rangers, and she surreptitiously walked up to show me something in her coat. As she got very close to me, she showed a stuffed fairy penguin that she was bringing over for my perusal. Obviously, she didn't want to hold it in her hands because it would have led to all sorts of confusion as people surged to get close to her and children wailed to have a chance to touch this facsimile of one of the penguins.

As the penguin parade passed the onlookers, the birds ambled toward their nests, some as far as a kilometer away. The preserve has constructed boardwalks with lights almost like little streetlights so viewers can follow individual penguins as these penguins go to their nests. I, too, got caught in the fairy magic of the penguins. Nancy and I followed one to its burrow. I enjoyed listening to its flat feet hitting the sand and its little wings batting against its sides. At one point the penguin stopped along his journey and seemed to heave out a sigh, apparently tiring of this nightly ritual. How this little bird must have been befuddled by the fact that thousands of people have traveled several hours from cities like Melbourne to see this nightly odyssey.

Another place of great risk--economic risk--must be the entire complex surrounding Ayers Rock (also known by its native name –

Uluru). One of the interesting things I first learned about the Rock was that it isn't all that close to Alice Springs. The Rock is located a little over two hundred miles from Alice Springs and is really in the middle of nowhere since Alice Springs itself is in the middle of nowhere. However, despite this fact, a gigantic commercial support center has been built a small distance from the Rock. This commercial support center includes an airport, shuttle buses, four hotels, a shopping area, and a campground. In addition to the accommodations for the tourists, there are also accommodations for the workers who provide the services here since there is no community nearby from which the workers could commute. Not only is there plenty of economic activity, but the economic activity is quite costly. Tourist rooms can range all the way to $1,500 per night! Nancy and I, of course, did not stay in this pricy resort but our room at the Lost Camel was listed to cost $300.

What drives tourists to go the great distances to the Rock and to pay the kind of prices I had mentioned? I guess I would have to say that the Rock has a magic and mystic magnetism of its own. I was surprised to find that the Rock is only the second largest monolith in the world. The largest rock monolith in the world is also in Australia but has not received the fame that Ayers Rock has. This fame has developed over the last century. I can't imagine what the early conversations about the Rock were like. Perhaps the best thing to do is to imagine a conversation that might have taken place between a seller of the Rock and a potential Buyer:

Seller. Well, you just can't miss this investment opportunity.

Buyer. What is it you want me to invest in?

Seller. Well, I've got this rock. It's a real steal.

Buyer. What's so great about it?

Seller. Well, it's very, very big.

Buyer. How big? Is it the biggest in the world?

Seller. Well, it's not the biggest rock.

Buyer. How high is it?

Seller. About a thousand feet.

Buyer. Than it's not even as high as the Rock of Gibraltar.

Seller. No, but it's got a great color.

Buyer. Oh, yeah.

Seller. It's a real red sometimes.

Buyer. Well, do you think people would come and see it?

Seller. Oh, sure.

Buyer. It's located in a convenient location, right?

Seller. Not exactly.

Buyer. What do you mean?

Seller. It's about a thousand miles in the Outback.

Buyer. You must be kidding!

Seller. No, listen to me. People are really going to want to visit it.

Buyer. Why?

Seller. Well, for one thing they're going to want to climb on it.

Buyer. Climb on it?

Seller. Once people see that you can climb to the top, there will be no stopping them from trying to get to the top.

Buyer. Is there a good path to the top?

Seller. No, that's what makes it so exciting. Part of the reason people will climb it is because it is difficult.

Buyer. Oh.

Seller. There's one more thing. What you're buying is larger than what you see. Only one third of the rock is visible; the other two-thirds are underground.

Buyer. I see.

Seller. So, what do you say? Are you ready to put down some cash for this once in a lifetime opportunity?

Buyer. Let me see if I can sum it up. You want me to buy a big rock that is in the middle of nowhere. It's not the biggest rock in the world and most of it is hidden. You want me to invest a small fortune to buy it because you think people will come to it so they can have the difficulty of climbing to the top. Is that about it?

Seller. Yes, you've got it about right.

Buyer. I guess I'll have to pass on this opportunity. By the way, I've got to get going now. There is a bloke down in Sydney who wants me to invest in a company that makes boards that people can ride on when they are in the shark infested waters of the ocean. He says these boards--he wants to call them surfboards-- will be a big hit. I don't know but I think there is more of a chance that people will swim among the sharks than will climb a rock that is a thousand miles in the desert.

While the Rock, the surfing business, and the penguin parade seemed to be moving along successfully, other risks aren't as clear in their outcomes. One case that comes to my mind almost immediately occurred in the Barossa Valley, a prime wine country of Australia outside of Adelaide. The wine industry is doing quite well, but some other industries might not be sharing the same success. As Nancy and I were driving a deserted country road back to Adelaide, Nancy pointed out a truck and a man on the side of the road who was selling horse manure. We both laughed as we saw the horse manure for sale; since there were no—I mean no—other travelers on this road. What kind of expectations could this owner of the horse manure have or what sales could make it worth his time? Even if every car that passed along the road stopped, the horse manure could hardly provide adequate compensation for the time spent waiting for cars to stop. I wonder how many cars out of ten travel along a country road looking for horse manure, or how many would stop when the driver of the car saw that horse manure was for sale! Like the nature of the Divine Trinity, this is a mystery I will never be able to solve.

Another venture that poses a great deal of business risk is the construction of BIG things in the middle of nowhere. This is an Australian fascination that is a lot of fun even though I'm not sure how profitable it is. As Nancy and I drove along the Australian countryside, Nancy kept her eye out for any BIG thing. We knew from our research that there was a BIG lobster, a BIG banana, a BIG rocking horse, and a BIG pineapple along with other BIG things. Our first BIG adventure was our encounter with the BIG lobster outside of Kingston, Australia. There is not much population around Kingston; in fact, there is not much population in Kingston. The lobster sits outside the town about a kilometer away, in the middle of very arid farmland. There was not much traffic on this road. Although compared to the road that the horse manure salesman was on, this road seemed like an LA freeway. When we saw the BIG lobster about fifty-five feet high on a hill on the side of the road, I got very excited. The stupidity of it all really appealed to me. As we drove into the parking lot, the only other car in view was driving out. We parked and took the obligatory pictures, and these gave me an opportunity to feel the whacky side of the lobster. The lobster was red so it not only was a BIG lobster but it was a BIG cooked lobster. Inside the lobster were a café and a gift shop. I got an idea of the profitability of the lobster when I talked to the single employee who was in evidence. She was working the cash register and was about seventy years old. As I chatted her up, she revealed that she was one of the co-owners and was seriously seeking a new buyer for the lobster. She informed me that ownership of such a tourist attraction was not all that one might fantasize it would be. Nancy and I had not yet been to Ayers Rock, so I wasn't able to offer the business point that the lobster would become more successful if she constructed a difficult climb to the top. This would surely fascinate the visitors. We purchased a couple of postcards that probably doubled the sales for the day and went back to our drive along the deserted highway.

As Nancy and I drove along, we mused about the entrepreneurial spirit of the Australians. In Kingston itself the citizenry had showed themselves entrepreneurs and as people who would attempt to make lemonade out of lemon juice. Kingston is a region of sinkholes. Now, most people, when they hear the word sinkhole, imagine a place that might not do that well in terms of prosperity. However, the large sinkhole right in the middle of Kingston has become a tourist attraction for the town--although I must say it's not a BIG tourist attraction even though it is a BIG sinkhole. What the good citizens of Kingston have done is to create a large garden area at the bottom of the sinkhole. Cleverly, getting to this garden involves an inconvenient climb down and up some stairs. Of course, this adds to the tourist excitement to visit the garden in the sinkhole.

As I think about the inhabitants of New Zealand and Australia, I can't help but think of optimistic people buoyant on a sea of risk. Like the surfers we often associate with these people, they seem able to take the risk for the ride of a lifetime. Another way of looking at it is that risk is like oxygen in New Zealand and Australia. It's part of what gives life to these places. There are risky animals; there are risky geological and climatic features, and there is an optimistic risk-taking capacity in the people. Like oxygen, the risk can be dangerous and cause things to flame up more intensely and possibly ignite. On the other hand, like oxygen, the riskiness of New Zealand and Australia give experience a great deal of life.

GRIPING ABOUT GROUPS

Nancy and I spent seventy of the seventy-two days we were in New Zealand and Australia on what is called a self-guided tour. A company called Abel-Tasman Tours booked all of our room accommodations and car rentals several months in advance. When we left on our trip, we left with a book of vouchers. Vouchers would be turned in for our rooms and vehicles when we reached our destinations in New Zealand and Australia. Because we were dealing with a tour company, we seemed to get some pretty good deals on the rooms we had. In fact, at times we had rooms that by our standards were simply luxurious, yet the price was still in the economy range. Only two of our days were in a traditional tour format; these were our days on Kangaroo Island. While the tour personnel on Kangaroo Island were fine, these two days reminded me of what makes group travel something I usually try to avoid.

The first thing is the ridiculous hour that the tour usually gets its clients up and going. In our case, the tour bus picked us up at 6:00 A.M.! To have any chance of making this rendezvous with any clothes on, Nancy and I had to be up by 5:30 A.M. I know the tours want us to see as much as possible, but I'm sure there is something that can be left out.

Once we got started, we faced an unexpectedly long bus ride from Adelaide to the point where the ferry would leave for Kangaroo Island. This bus trip of two hours could have been time for people to relax and perhaps take a little nap. Unfortunately, something caused a problem here--another passenger. The guilty party happened to be a girl about eighteen years of age. From the moment she got on the bus, all she could do was talk and talk and talk. She had come on the bus with another young woman who was just learning English. This second woman, because of her limited English, didn't feel comfortable in speaking and so our talker proceeded to fill in any quiet time with her very annoying ramblings. I have to give the gal some credit however. I have never run into anyone who could talk nonstop for two hours and say absolutely nothing. What she did was to tell the non-English speaker everything that happened in her life over the last half year almost as if she were reading an agenda of things that she did--getting up, brushing her teeth, going to buy a greeting card, etc. were all part of this mindless recitation of nothingness. Unlike a diary, there was absolutely no insight or reflection in these comments. Because she was young, the girl had enough physical energy to keep her voice at a sufficiently high level to make sure it reached as many of the other passengers as possible. To make matters worse, the rest of the passengers on the bus were very quiet. The only redeeming aspect of this girl's rattle is that she was not doing it on a cell phone.

The other people in the group, of course, are always the wild cards. Nancy has traveled in groups on several occasions when I did not accompany her on her trips. She is diligent in planning, and so she reads very closely the recommendations and suggestions that come from the tour operator. As she prepared for her trip to Russia, Nancy read to me of the clear requirement for the tour she was taking. All members of the group needed to able to walk several miles and also be able to handle their own luggage. As anyone who studies human behavior might have guessed, there were people who showed up on her tour who had problems breathing without bottled oxygen and others who had suitcases which were so big that it would take a crane to move them. As might be expected, these people caused problems when movement became necessary. To make matters worse, the very people who caused the problems would complain about the very problems they were having.

On our trip to Kangaroo Island, I did not hear the clanging of oxygen bottles, but Nancy and I did run into some problems with people who could not follow directions. Following directions, of course, is something that involves listening, something that is hard to do if one is talking all the time. One case I remember distinctly involved a rather sophisticated European woman on the trip who certainly had enough English to understand what was going on but just didn't seem to care to follow the directions that had been given. We were on a beach where there were scores of sea lions. Some of the males of this herd could be very imposing indeed and weighed up to six hundred pounds. Before we descended to the beach, the park ranger said very slowly and carefully that we should not get very close to the sea lions and should give them a good deal of distance. He repeated the notion several times that we maintain at least ten meters between us and these impressive mammals. Nancy couldn't believe it when this woman strolled over, getting closer and closer to a sea lion until the sea lion became a bit agitated. The violation of his territory had caused him to want to respond. Because of this silly lady's thoughtlessness, the ranger had to move the entire group very quickly and carefully from any proximity with this now disturbed beast. What made this woman think that she knew better? As travelers, Nancy and I had seen this behavior many times, although I still have trouble trying to figure it out. At one of the wildlife refuges we visited, there was a clear sign that said, "Do not feed the kangaroos." It did not say feed the kangaroos on Monday, Tuesday and Friday, it said, "Do not feed the kangaroos." Yet amazingly enough, Nancy observed a woman grabbing some leaves from the side of the path and feeding it to the kangaroo. Nancy noted that the sign did not say "… except when you pick the leaves at the side of the path."

When people behave like jerks, I always wonder what I should do. I could confront them, but what are the chances that they are going to admit to the stupidity I have clearly outlined? In addition, I am not a big fan of confrontation. It is not a pleasant experience for me as it is for others. Usually I have come on a trip to enjoy myself and not to confront others. I think it would be wonderful if the people who are running the tour would become more dictatorial. In fact, I think there should be a special place on the bus that is located in the back opposite the bathroom. If people are acting like grammar school children, I think they should be treated as such. A closet-type room without windows might be the perfect place for some who would have the time to consider how they are disturbing others while they are ensconced in this tour bus penalty box. After a warning to a person that he or she was talking much too loudly and disturbing others, the driver would lead the individual into the closet where the person would stay for a couple of hours. I would not expect that the guilty party would have to wear a tall pointed hat, although this could be an option for second and third offenses. I'm also not sure whether one such closet of shame would be enough. On trips I've taken from Cortland to New York City, there have been numerous boneheaded cell phone users who used the opportunity of traveling on the bus to call every acquaintance they have ever known and to share these conversations as loudly as they can with other travelers on the bus. Although I've heard the drivers sometimes threaten passengers with punishment for this annoying inconsideration, I still have not witnessed a passenger being put off the bus.

Some of the people I know are willing to travel in groups because they don't want to deal with the details involved in traveling. For Nancy and me dealing with the details is part of the experience. In fact, dealing with the details makes the trip a longer enjoyment than it might be. Usually Nancy spends several months doing research on the places we are visiting, and I get involved in making many decisions about which options we should select. I feel that as we make our decisions and make our day-to-day trip plans, we really get to know a place. Since we usually allow a lot of time for our travel, we have a great deal of flexibility if something unusual happens. It is certainly more work for us to work as we do, but I think we get much more out of our traveling experiences.

IMP-RESSIONS

If I were doing a survey of what people fear most traveling by plane, I can think of several responses that I surely could count on. I'm sure that people would express fear of terrorism and the possibility of the plane crashing. In addition to that, I'm sure people would have a fear of losing their luggage. This would be quite an inconvenience when they reached their destination. Then again, some people would be quite concerned and have fears, perhaps rational or perhaps irrational, about whether or not the supply of peanuts or pretzels in the small bags would run out. After all, in our modern transportation system, these peanuts and pretzels are the only food that is available for free. However, if I were doing a survey of a particularly thoughtful group, I am certain that their number one fear and the most prominent phobia and the most diabolical and sinister enemy of the traveling public is children!

These pirates of peace strip the airplane cabin of all its serenity. Babies and toddlers scream at all times of the day and night as if they were being flagellated alive by their parents while their wounds were being treated with the most acidic vinegar. Plane size makes no difference. A small plane is quickly filled with the shrieks of the young. A larger plane--possibly a space more difficult to fill with the volume of noise--is also filled with the prospect of more and more children. Children between the ages of five and ten are not much better. They yell and cry out with a vocal force that would make even an opera singer envious. They argue with their parents and kick vigorously into the back of the seat that is in front of them. This by the way is the seat that I'm usually sitting in. In addition, the older children are mobile. They enjoy running up and down the aisles. It's even more fun when the seatbelt sign is on. My fellow passengers and I just wait until that moment of a little bit of turbulence bounces the child off balance and brings a forehead or a mouth crashing down on a seat armrest; then the fun really begins.

Bringing children on planes isn't a bad idea; it's a horrible idea! Yet, the presence of so many children on so many planes suggests that many parents have not yet had the epiphany about the horror of bringing children onto a plane. Why is this? I think there are two answers. First, many parents feel guilty about bringing children into the world and not spending much time with them during the year. To some, childbearing is a part of life like getting a driver's license or going to the prom. A commitment to childbearing is much different from a commitment to parenting. As a result, there is considerable guilt. The guilt needs to go somewhere; it goes to thirty thousand feet. A second reason a parent would take a child on a plane is the delusion that the child is well-behaved. Many parents don't know what a well-behaved child is like and do not look objectively at the little bundle of joy that they brought into the world in a realistic way. Perhaps a view of the genesis of my thoughts might help a few of these parents.

The standards for a well-behaved child were formed in my youth, for as the reader might guess, I was a well-behaved child. The first thing is that a well-behaved child knows that he is not the center of the universe; his parents are. A few objective measures might help. When I was a child, my mother would occasionally signal me to come and be near her. Unlike the modern parents, she did not have to yell and scream to get me by her side. What my mother did was to look in my direction, and with the index finger on her right hand, point at me then curl it back toward herself. She would curl that finger just two or three times, and I would immediately head her way. There was no talk; there was no discussion; there was no consideration whether I felt that this was a reasonable command. I looked, and I obeyed. My behavior was not modeled after that of a free-range chicken. Psychobabble had not been invented yet so there was no talk of "exploring my limits" or "assessing my power against authority figures." Such excuses for bad behavior were a decade or two away. I was my mother's representative in public, and I would not under any circumstances disturb others and bring shame upon the family. There were times, however, when I would be doing something on my own. At these times it was uncommon for me to go beyond what I had already developed confidence about in terms of proper behavior. At these moments when I was doing something I wasn't sure of, I would glance at my mother. I could be fairly sure that she had one eye in my direction at all times. Well-behaved children, after all, do not spring out of the ground like petunias. When I caught my mother's eye and she observed what I was doing, she would immediately access the appropriateness of my behavior. If the behavior happened to be fine, she gave no indication. If, however, my behavior was not appropriate, my mother would very subtlety move her head back and forth to signal no. Just this slight movement of her head one or two times to the left and to the right would stop me in my tracks every time.

At school my mother's work was reinforced by the good Sisters of St. Joseph. The good behavior of young Christian boys and girls was important to them, and they took their work seriously. Mother Superior represented the height of behavioral education. She performed feats which today would seem beyond the pale of the imagination. When we attended church, she controlled about four or five hundred children between the ages of five and thirteen. All Mother Superior had in her possession to accomplish this great task was a frog clicker and her fingers. We marched silently into church, and with the sound of the frog clicker all four hundred of us would genuflect and at the sound of the next click rise in our pews. When the next click occurred, we would either kneel or sit down depending on what was gong on in the religious service. When we were in other assemblies, Mother Superior would walk around the perimeter of the student body and with eyes that seemed to move like modern radar peruse and analyze the behaviors of all the students present. She was totally aware of what was going on in every seat occupied by every student in the assembly. If she saw something that was amiss, she would look intently in the direction of the possible infraction and just snap her fingers. At this point usually the offending party would just look at her, and she would do the horizontal head movement that had been made famous by my mother. If the child did not respond in the proper manner, seeing that the behavior was offensive, Mother Superior would break the spell and snap her fingers. Once catching the child's attention, she would use the index finger curl indicating that the child was to report to her side immediately. This always worked. As I look back at the education I received from the nuns and my mother, it is clear why I was a well-behaved child. The down side, of course, from these experiences was that I developed the idea that all children should be well-behaved and in fact were well-behaved. My first commercial flight proved how significant an error I had made.

There are, of course, solutions for the problem I am describing. Certainly there could be days indicated when children under thirteen can travel. I would suggest that these days be Wednesdays and Saturdays. Everyone else could travel any day of the week, but if one traveled on a Wednesday or Saturday with children on the plane, he would know that he would have to say to himself that the children had a right to be there that day and part of the responsibility was his own. Another possible solution for the problem of children on aircraft actually seems to be in the process of development. I understand that some of the new larger planes now being planned include a play area similar to those at McDonald's. Surely, if there were to be a play area, that area would have to be enclosed in some sort of soundproof glass. Having a section of seats surrounded by soundproof glass for those traveling with children seems to me an idea that is long overdue.

Finally I have a solution of my own that I have not been able to develop because of technological and financial limitations. It would go like this. I would like someone to design a helmet that can be placed on the shoulders of the child. This helmet--something like an inverted fish bowl--would be made of soundproof, yet transparent material. Oxygen would be provided, of course, for this helmet and a microphone would be placed inside the device with a volume control on the back that could easily be turned higher or lower by an adult but would be difficult for a child to reach. Once the helmet was in position, the child could look around but could not be heard except at a volume permitted by the parent. Such a device would render children's screams and cries just a sad memory of a problem-ridden past.

The terror of poorly behaved children on airplanes is significant because the poor passengers have no place to go to escape. The situation in restaurants is not quite as desperate, but it is still significant. Now I don't mean restaurants like McDonald's and Burger King; these are the natural habitat of children in the feeding process. Anyone who expects quiet in these places is delusional. When I enter one of these establishments, I know I am on someone else's turf. However, when I am in a place that dispenses alcoholic beverages and lunch items start at $10, I think it is reasonable to assume that my dining experience will be somewhat civilized.

The fact that my assumptions are often incorrect was clearly displayed when Nancy and I decided to have lunch at Noosa Junction, Australia. Nancy and I were looking for a particularly romantic event. We checked out several menus and decided one particular restaurant had both the cuisine and view that we wanted. We had a lovely table over the river and we settled in a romantic tête-à-tête. We had barely tasted a sip or two of wine and a bit of our salad, when we heard the unmistakable whining and crying of a poorly behaved imp. Accompanied by two parents or two grandparents (both can be equally bad at keeping an imp at bay), the child was already acting up, and hadn't sat down at the table yet. Sometimes overhead music and loud conversations from other tables can help to mask the sound of a poorly behaved child. This was not the case on this day in what had been a very serene and civilized restaurant. Now the bad decision of the adults was going to affect our enjoyment of our meal. To anyone with a scintilla of intelligence, it would have been clear that the child was an inappropriate placement at this restaurant. However, instead of facing this rather obvious fact, the adults began either to argue with the child or to ignore it. Neither strategy was going to make the situation any better. Although I prayed to Marcus Aurelius for a stoic response to this inconsideration that was taking place a few tables from me, my prayers were not answered. Nancy too felt bad about what had been imposed upon us.

Besides praying, I wondered what else I could do. If I asked the people to leave the restaurant, I doubted that they would do so. If they responded to my request with insults, I don't know where the escalation might lead. Pouring Ranch dressing on their heads might not have a calming effect. The truth, as my reader already knows, is that I'm not confrontational. I go to a restaurant not to confront other diners; I go to enjoy my food in peace.

I guess the point of all of this is that I would like to begin a dialogue among all travelers concerning consideration for all others. The fact that one has a child does not give the parent a license to annoy. Unlike

James Bond whose 007 designation gave him a license to kill wherever and whenever he pleased, parents of children do not have an 00C designation that gives them a license to annoy other people wherever and whenever they wish. To have a child is a big responsibility; part of this responsibility includes having consideration for other human beings as well as making sure that the child who is developing will become himself a considerate and non-annoying human.

I might just be spitting in the wind on this. Looking for well-behaved children and considerate parents might be like looking for a good-tasting hamburger without cholesterol or a robust beer that actually helps one lose weight. Nonetheless, someone must speak out. The emperor has no clothes, and the eight hundred pound gorilla in the living room is wrecking the television set. I can't imagine what kind of bedlam will occur in the new airbus 380 when 40 of its 800 passengers happen to be children under five. Even though the French and British were able to join together to build the Concorde aircraft, I doubt they'll be able to establish any cabin concord on this new jetliner of theirs. Oh well, maybe I should just listen to an audio book of Marcus Aurelius.

ODDITIES FOR AN ENDING

In terms of the travel vehicle metaphor that began this book, I have driven to and visited all the major points of my trips. I tried to avoid taking side trips, but I know from experience that some of these side trips might be of interest to my reading passenger. Now, as I'm heading home, I find that I have a small bit of time that I can use to take my literary friends to a few out of the way places that might be interesting and exciting. I promise that these stops will be brief, and my passengers, if they choose, can even stay in the car. However, I encourage my passengers to come along with me, for if my past experiences are any indicator, some of these side trips might prove to be among my most memorable experiences.

WHATEVER HAPPENED TO THE OTHER FOUR APOSTLES?

Driving along the Great Ocean Highway is one of the must-do's for any Australian traveler. Before I can comment on what someone must see on this highway, I have to comment on the names of roads in Australia. In general, I think that it is fair to say that the signage is horrible. I can only imagine that the Australians hired consultants from New Jersey to put up the road signs. Nancy and I had the pleasure of driving along the Great Western Highway as well as the Western Highway. I suppose that if we travel in the country a bit more we would have experienced the Mediocre Western Highway and the Pretty Good Western Highway. In any event, Nancy told me that the scenery across the Great Ocean Highway is not only breathtaking, it is suffocating. In fact, for many travelers along this road the scenery is confusing because with every twist and turn in the road the next vantage point offers an even more spectacular view than the previous one, and it is hard to believe that such scenic splendor can keep outdoing itself. The climax of this ocular opulence occurs in an area that is known for The Twelve

Apostles. These Apostles are natural rock formations that rise out of the sea. Their dramatic presence as large waves break against them hypnotizes tourists who watch them from the shore. Unfortunately, there are no longer twelve of these rock formations--as far as any tourist can view them. Nancy and I--well, Nancy--counted eight. Six were on one side of our lookout point, and two were on the other side. What happened to the other four? Was Judas one of them? Did the other three run off with Judas? In truth, what occurred was the result of the fact that the sea is not very good about the maintenance of tourist attractions. Mother Nature is not Walt Disney. Over the years the ocean has destroyed four of the rock formations. While Nancy and I were told that the remnants of the rock columns were still standing under the surface of the waves, we had not brought along our submarine. I think a contest should be setup to rename the Apostles and recognize that only eight of them still exist. My nominee is to call the remaining eight columns the "Ocular Eight."

Though there are only eight Apostles, travelers come by the thousands to see them. The Australians, as usual, are wonderfully obliging with viewing platforms. One thing, however, that drives me crazy is the constant presence of helicopters. One doesn't have to see everything from a whirly bird. Nonetheless, helicopters generate considerable income for their owners, and tourists, rightly or wrongly, believe that they can only have the fullest tourist experience if they engage in some vision from above. For me, the view from above has never been consistent with the expense. When I used to see, I was often disappointed in aircraft flights because the scenery I was viewing didn't seem all that spectacular. Viewed from above, scenery loses its vertical dimension. As a result, what seemed very interesting from the ground has become very flat from above. But, I'm surely out of the mainstream, for when Nancy and I were at the Apostles, helicopters zoomed and dove overhead like a swarm of mosquitoes, making a disturbing racket that was only somewhat muted by the crashing of the great sea waves against the rocks.

DELIGHTING THE DISABLED

Driving on the road to Rotorua, Nancy pointed out a sign to me: "Horseback Riding for the Disabled." Now I know that these activities are setup with the best of intentions. Yet, I somehow get the idea that people think that every last disabled person on the planet really wants to get on a horse. They imagine all sorts of disabled people with ear-to-ear smiles on their faces riding around in circles or in straight lines and having the time of their lives. Some do, and that's great. However, although I like to bet on horses, I have absolutely no interest in riding one. By putting this fact on the table that all disabled people are not interested in riding horses, maybe I can assist the altruistic in expanding their helping horizons. If these people want to do something to delight the disabled, I would suggest the following. I would like to see a sign that read: "Free Happy Hour for the Disabled--any hour of the day or night." Now we're talking!

WHAT PRICE INTOXICANTS?

As I mentioned earlier, the price of wine can be somewhat high in Australia. In fact, all beverages that contain alcohol have a rather significant price tag, and this is surprising in a country that has a romantic reputation for being wild and wooly. When I came to Australia, I had the notion that beer and spirits were going to be treated in a manner similar to bread; they were going to be universally available and offered at very low prices. This was not the case. Although I could usually get a pint of beer at a pub for three or four dollars, a case of beer at a retail shop would cost between $25 and $33. This was more than double what I would pay in New York State, a state not known for its friendliness to consumers. In a bottle shop in Yeppoon, I decided to research the topic and asked one of the employees of the shop why prices were so high. He told me that the tax on alcoholic beverages was forty-one percent! The Australian Socialists had apparently found an alcoholic cash cow to milk.

THE PRICE OF FREEDOM

I'm sure a few of my readers are probably interested in the cost of our motor home trip from Cairns to Brisbane. The Mercedes-Benz diesel did surprisingly well on gas mileage and averaged about 18 miles per gallon. To put this in perspective, I want to point out that the motor home that Nancy and I had in the United States got ten to eleven miles per gallon. Our U.S. motor home was gasoline powered and was not at all streamlined as our Australian vehicle although it was just as long. In April of 2007, the cost for a gallon of fuel in Australia was between $4.10 and $4.20 in American currency. In our two-week trip we used approximately 70 gallons of fuel. If we assumed that fuel in 2007 was selling for about $3.10 in the U.S., our Australian cost was only $70 more than we would have paid in the U.S. Another way to look at it is that if the price in the U.S. was $2.10, we still would have only paid $140 more than we might have with that low price of fuel in the U.S. This would amount to only ten dollars per day on our two-week trip. Obviously, such a cost would have been negligible in a trip such as ours. In addition, to put fuel prices in perspective, I would like to point out that on a trip in 2006 to the Costa Brava in Spain we paid $5 for a gallon of fuel. Interestingly, the roads in Australia and Spain were full of drivers going about their business. The hysteria that the media in the U.S. likes to whip up which consumes many Americans, did not seem to be present at all in Spain or Australia. I'm not sure whether I need to be outraged at the American media or ashamed of my fellow citizens or both.

FOOD FLIGHTS

Before I begin a random discussion of food in Australia, I must present a disclaimer. I have a very broad tolerance for all types and tastes of foods. In truth, Nancy is the same way. In college the two of us were among the few that looked forward to the meals in the dining hall. While we can recognize and appreciate gourmet meals, neither Nancy nor I have much interest in paying for them. This lack of interest in paying gourmet prices is intensified by the fact that very often what is touted as "gourmet" is not really "gourmet" at all. Nonetheless, I do feel qualified to share a few tidbits about food that might provide the reader with some insights about the general food offerings available in Australia.

If the only reason travelers went to Australia were to eat the food, the tourist trade would be sparse indeed. Unlike European countries such as Italy, France and Austria, Australian food, though edible, is not particularly noteworthy. To be sure, some of the main cities have seen an increase in the international cuisine available, but this alone would not justify a 10,000 mile food run to the Red Continent. Yet, having said this, like any country, Australia does have some variations in food preparation that are of some interest.

The first thing that struck me was the different way that Australians regard salad. Stopping for lunch in a café, I would be asked if I would like salad with my sandwich. I love salad. However, the Australians were not referring to a bowl of salad that I would get in addition to my sandwich; they were simply referring to some lettuce and tomato that they would put on my plate next to my sandwich or put on my sandwich itself. In short, the word "salad" meant lettuce and tomato would be provided.

Speaking of items that wind up on top of sandwiches, I should also bring up the lonely beet. In America we don't eat a lot of beets. Beets can be seen in clear glass jars in our grocery stores, but it is a rare shopping cart indeed that holds many of these glass containers. Beets are more often seen holding a place of distinction at a salad bar. They are relatively cheap and provide the function of potato salad, noodle salad and coleslaw. That is, they furnish filling fodder for the diner at the restaurant. In Australia, however, the beet is aristocracy and often finds itself as a topper for hamburgers. Amazingly, the beets have staged a coup and in many places in Australia had replaced the sliced onion as the topping of choice. Beets are not offensive, but as a replacement for sweet, sliced onions, they are about as effective as replacing Sean Connery in the James Bond role with Tim Conway.

Eating a healthy diet should also be important to the traveler. There are surely times to celebrate, but this time of celebration should not equate with every mealtime. Unfortunately, the Australians are a growing population--they are growing fatter and fatter everyday. Not only is it sad for the Australians, but it is also sad for the rest of the world, for we have had an image of the Australians as a fit and vibrant people. Now, however, growing affluence, two-career families, and the ubiquitous French fries and potato chips are taking their toll. Chips (French fries) and crisps (potato chips), are literally nasty villains. Although I rarely had chips with my meals, when I did have them, the piles of them on my plate were incredibly high. There were usually enough fries to satisfy--or overwhelm--three diners! In addition, fast food restaurants are everywhere. McDonald's, of course, is in every town and is often accompanied by Burger King although in Australia it operates under the alias of Hungry Jack. Kentucky Fried Chicken competes with Red Rooster, and Gloria Jean not only makes good coffee available but tempts the customer with a wide range of donuts, muffins and other pastries.

I would certainly be negligent if I did not warn the reader about an even more insidious friend of fat--the meat pie. This Australian staple once made some sense for a working class population that toiled long hours of hard physical labor and needed an inexpensive source of energy and sustenance. In a variety of meat flavors, a small meat pie packs an outstanding 700 calories into its tiny body. The irony is that the meat pie might be relatively small, but the impact it can have on making the eater BIG is quite substantial. These pies sell for $2-$3. Eating a few of these a week in moments of diet weakness surely can have explosive effects on the waistline.

Speaking of items that can put on the pounds, I can't omit a short discussion of pizza. Surprisingly, I found pizza to be nicely done in Australia although I only had it a few times. I would recommend trying a pizza "with the works," especially if these "works" include seafood. Nancy and I followed this strategy several times and were very pleased with the results. In Cairns the pizza we had delivered wound up giving us four meals! The abundance of toppings was such that one slice was more than enough for lunch and two slices at dinner made a monumental meal.

To keep costs down, Nancy and I often had breakfast in our hotel rooms. Many of these rooms had not only a refrigerator but also a microwave; in some instances we even had access to a small kitchen. Uncle Toby's instant oatmeal was not only inexpensive but tasty too. The cold cereal Museli came in a wide variety of flavors and usually included grains, nuts, and dried fruit. I got use to pouring hot water on the Museli and found that this kind of breakfast would keep me going right up to lunchtime.

Planning not to be hungry is certainly an important part of an economical vacation, to be sure. Nancy is a great one for always having a small snack on hand in the event that hunger strikes. One of the things that we both enjoyed on this trip was the bag of Spanish peanuts we always had with us. Arriving at our hotel in mid-afternoon as we often did, those Spanish peanuts would really save the day. As the situation in the Lost Camel showed very clearly, not having access to a snack and yet wanting one could be a very costly set of circumstances. At the mini-bar in our room at the Lost Camel, there were, of course, numerous items for sale, but the one that I will never forget was the half-cylinder of Pringle's potato chips that was for sale for $4.50! I don't care if the currency is American, Australian, or Cameroon, $4.50 is a lot to pay for a few potato chips.

For the coffee lover, Australia holds mixed blessings. As a continent Australia seems to have abandoned drip coffee for brewed coffee. They like a Starbuck's kind of flavor; unfortunately, they also seem comfortable with Starbuck's level of pricing. A cup of coffee costs about $3.00, and this is a fairly small cup. When one asks for a larger cup, the serving staff will almost always indicate that they have mugs of coffee. These mugs, however, are not much larger than the cup, and these mugs cost about $3.50. I found only two places where I routinely could find larger cups of coffee that I could have as take-away items (take-away is the Australian phrase for "to go"). Both McDonald's and the Gloria Jean coffee chain would provide sixteen ounce cups of coffee to go. These were only slightly more expensive than a much smaller mug of coffee. To compete with its coffee shop rivals, McDonald's has introduced a specialty café section where the coffee is better and there are other delicacies and pastries to tempt the customer.

Because Nancy and I often take long trips like this 72-day trip to Australia and New Zealand, we had to find ways to economize. One fun way that we did this is that we would sometime take a meal at a supermarket. While the ambiance is sometimes limited, the values are quite often noteworthy. Sometimes the food is not half bad. In Adelaide we had a rather amusing experience. It was lunchtime, and we found a delicatessen--café attached to a supermarket. Nancy and I both ordered sandwiches but I also wanted coleslaw. I asked the clerk for a portion of coleslaw, thinking I was going to get the typical side dish of coleslaw. Apparently, the clerk misunderstood me and gave me a portion of coleslaw that would feed six people. Since the coleslaw ended up costing more than my sandwich, this wasn't exactly the kind of budget operation that Nancy and I had planned for that day. As I labored to finish my coleslaw, I heard another customer go up to the counter and order a sandwich that she wanted on a particular kind of bread. The clerk responded that she only had one kind of bread. I found this totally ridiculous. Here the clerk was in a café that was part of a grocery store! Couldn't she just go into the store or call on the phone to get any kind of bread that she wanted brought over to the café section? Apparently this thought never struck her. Such incredibly poor customer service is always a wonder to me. Why not make customers happy when it would have been so easy to do so?

<u>LOVE LETTERS IN THE SAND</u>

Travel companies love to conjure up business by marketing romantic fantasies. One of the most common fantasies is the one where a couple walks alone along a romantic and deserted beach. With the population of the world approaching seven billion, such deserted beaches are becoming harder and harder to find and thus becoming greater and greater fantasies. On the Queensland Coast, Nancy and I had the opportunity to experience a deserted beach; it was no fantasy. We had gotten off the highway several hundred miles from any population center. We noted that there were homes for sale in this area, but they were much less expensive than the ones we had seen near the population centers. We parked our motor home at a playground parking lot and proceeded for a walk on the beach. We passed three people--an older gentlemen and two children--playing in the surf in the confines of a protective net. After passing these people, we proceeded to take a long walk, a walk during which we saw and heard no other human beings. When the net and its inhabitants were quite out of sight, I realized that Nancy and I were quite alone. At least I thought we were alone. Instead of trying to kiss my lovely wife--something that would always happen in the romantic fantasies--I began to scan the area with my highly sensitive hearing. As I listened, I could sense that there was plenty of brush and foliage past the dunes where anyone who wished to hide could conceal himself. Then again, Australia was full of animals. What would Nancy and I do if a big dog confronted us; even worse, what would Nancy and I do if a pack of big dogs confronted us? As I listened, I was frustrated by the muting effect of the crashing of the waves and the humming of the vigorous shore breeze on my ears and hearing acuity. Was I being overly cautious? Perhaps I was; perhaps I wasn't. Like that moment in Harvey's Bay when I began to worry about the sharks, I was beginning to feel a little uncomfortable and exposed. I suggested to Nancy that it was time to turn around, and once again she complied with my wishes. I was glad to get back to the motor home where I had time to consider the full ramifications of isolation.

We had a much more romantic time on a catamaran that we took for a sail around Sydney Harbor. I was quite happy to get on a ship with sails. Like so many armchair sailors, I have developed quite a romance about the sea and the era of wooden ships and iron men. On this trip the memory of Captain Cook and his sailing ship Endeavor were constantly on my mind. Two and half centuries after his magnificent navigational exploits, I'm still astonished by the skill and courage he brought to his exploration of the Pacific and the land down under. In our case, our large catamaran left the dock under diesel power. However, once we had maneuvering room, the captain cut the engines and lowered the sails. The tilt of the ship, the creaking of the rigging, and the insistent pushing forward of the ship by a light breeze filled my spirit with the romance of the seas. This romance and the relative quiet of our classic propulsion system must have affected the other passengers as well, for the conversational noise sank to the level of a church confessional. Indistinct murmurings replaced rowdy and oafish conversations. Best of all, no one activated or responded to a cell phone. Surrounded by the splendor of this great city of the 21st century, we glided in the glory of transportation from the 18th century. It was a moment to treasure.

YOUNG AUSTRALIAN RENEGADES

Because of Australia's long association with the British Commonwealth, I assumed that its citizens would be the best behaved in the world in terms of propriety and following rules. England is, of course, the home of the queue, that magical line of human beings that seems to form whenever order is needed. In my mind the queue is one sure thing that separates human beings from monkeys. If monkeys and humans are almost alike in DNA, the one area of genetic incompatibility that surely exists is the presence of the queue genes in humans and its absence in chimpanzees. To queue is to be courteous; to queue is to think; to queue is to be a gentleman. Thinking this way, I was quite surprised to hear what was going on in some campgrounds during the

Easter holiday. Everyone it seems wants to go on holiday in Australia. While there are many parks and campgrounds in Australia, there are not enough sites to serve everyone if the entire population wanted to go at the same time. Planning for the holiday and reserving a site seemed to be the necessary requirement for Easter holiday happiness. Now, I don't want to demean young people, but I often find that their notion of reality is somewhat fanciful. When it comes to camping, I have often found that young people expect to get the best sites--those nearest the water--at the least expensive prices. In addition, they expect that these sites will be available with no advance booking. Such indeed were the conditions that came together for the Easter holiday of 2007. When thousands of young dreamers decided to go on holiday, they found out that there were no places for them at the public campgrounds. At the campgrounds, rangers and security people were there looking for permits and registration documents to maintain order. I was shocked to learn that many of the dreamers entered a campground and setup on a site in spite of the fact that they had not stopped in at the registration office and had no permits. I was astounded by others who setup their camping equipment and then presented permits to rangers for sites in other campgrounds! As reader can imagine, the permit that some young campers had was not for some of the more desirable sites or campgrounds in Australia. It was like someone popping in to the Presidential Suite at the Plaza Hotel, New York City with a registration confirmation for the Comfort Inn in Secaucus. In spite of all this unruly behavior, the rangers and security people were able to sort things out without any significant destruction or turmoil. As I thought about these events, I realized that I should not have been so surprised. The ancestors of many of these prevaricators might not have had a very high queue quotient; they may in fact have been those original members of Australia's European community that came as the prisoners of the Botany Bay penal colony.

WHO STOLE THE U?

Over the years many people in the United States have wondered about the name of the Australian airline Qantas. What they wonder about is why the name of the airline does not have a U after the Q. They speculate that perhaps Qantas is an aboriginal word or a term from some South Pacific dialect. The truth is that it's not any word from any exotic language or dialect; it's an acronym. The letters in Qantas stand for Queensland and North Territory Air Service. Once I found out this information, I slept a lot better at night.

The Anti-Chamber of Commerce

I'm a strong believer in first impressions, whether these first impressions are in literature or in personal relationships. In my own case enthusiasm, friendliness, interest and competence are all qualities I try to put forward whenever I meet people. I am solidly in the camp of those people who believe that our first impressions of a place are important too. The quality and appearance of an airport, bus terminal, or a train station sends an important message to the traveler. On this score the airport at Alice Springs with its flies and excessive bathroom odors does not offer a very positive first impression as neither does the bus stations in Binghamton, New York or Cortland, New York. The inhabitants of the place are also part of the first impression. Taxi drivers and tour bus operators would certainly be very important elements of the first impression. I would expect that these people would be among the most significant purveyors of the first impression since they are in the hospitality business. However, in both Brisbane and Sydney Nancy and I ran into individuals who seemed to be not so much advocates for their cities but adversaries.

After dropping off our motor home in Brisbane, we were picked up by a cab that was in very good order. I don't know what kind of car I was riding in, but it was large, clean, and well equipped. We had a rather long ride to our hotel in the center of the city, so I decided to open a conversation with the driver in order to find out tidbits from him about what places in the city a native of Brisbane might suggest to a tourist. When I asked what he would recommend for us to do in Brisbane, he paused and finally said that there wasn't much to do in the city. In a rather odd way, he seemed rather stumped by the question. After a good deal of time, he finally responded to me more specifically and said that if we wanted, we could go to a particular mountain that overlooked the city and get a nice view of the city from there; it was a place where the satellite dishes for telecommunication were situated. Aside from this, he said that he really couldn't recommend anything!

When a few more minutes had passed, he told us that there was a casino in the city (Australians love to gamble), but it was probably the worst casino in the world. He continued on with his degradation of the casino and told us that the builders and operators of the casino should be ashamed of themselves for offering to the public such a tawdry, horrible place like the Brisbane casino. As an added thought he told us that if we wanted a good casino experience, we should leave town and head down the Gold Coast to a casino that was worth attending--the Jupiter Casino. Fortunately for Nancy and me we did not pay much attention to the negative utterances of this sour cab driver. We found Brisbane to be a charming place with many good restaurants and friendly pubs. Apparently, we had gotten an emissary from the Chamber of Horrors rather than the Chamber of Commerce.

When Nancy and I enter cities, we often look for a tour bus that will provide a guided tour of the city and in several hours point out to us the general places of interest that the city has to offer. While I digest the historical and political information these tours inevitably provide, Nancy absorbs all of the geographical information that is presented and integrates it with the information she has already stored from the very impressive map research she has done. I never traveled with anyone, male or female, who is able to identify the location and relationships faster than Nancy. During our stay in Auckland we had taken the city tour and were delighted with how it met our expectations. In Sydney, however, the experience was not so positive. Although the cost of the Explorer bus in Sydney was rather pricy, Nancy and I had had so many positive experiences on tours like this that we decided to pay the price. Unfortunately, our driver seemed to be working about fifteen years past his retirement period. He exhibited a strange and savage sarcasm. When passengers left the bus, he would sneer, "Have a nice day." While the words were the usual mindless pleasantry uttered by all of us, his tone, attitude, and distaste for the passengers he was serving were all quite obvious. Clearly, everything about his work disgusted him--the job itself, the city he was introducing, and the people he met. At first, many of us on the bus chuckled at his words. Surely, this must be an act. After awhile however, it sadly set in on all of us that this was no act. The mixture of the very positive tone of the recorded material of the tour and the extremely negative comments of the driver made our passage on this bus a very schizophrenic experience indeed.

Just so I don't leave this section on a negative note, I would like to mention a person who gave one of the greatest performances I have ever witnessed in the hospitality industry. What was so outstanding about this individual was that he gave great service not only to Nancy and me but to every person who came into contact with him. This was the reception clerk at the Lost Camel Hotel. Guests from this hotel come from all over the world. In general, when they reach this hotel that serves the resort of Ayers Rock, the guests are tired, confused about how they can best enjoy this resort and Ayers Rock, and somewhat unsure about how to pay for their accommodations in the most efficient manner. What this clerk did that was so remarkable is that he treated every guest as if that guest was the first and only guest that he was going to meet that day in the hotel. As I sat in the lobby and listened to his interactions, I realized that he worked a shift for twelve hours each day. Yet, even after seven or eight hours, as I listened to him, I could hear the same kind of enthusiasm in welcoming a guest, the same kind of patient listening and understanding that he gave to each guest, and the same kind of warm friendliness and good cheer. Whereas in Sydney we had a driver sent by the devil, at the Lost Camel we had a reception clerk who was a gift of the gods.

A Final Remark

These were just some of the experiences that gave our trip a tremendous amount of variability and interest. What I like about self-guided travel is that everyday seems to be an adventure. Because we had placed ourselves in this adventure, Nancy and I often had to solve problems. Now the word "problem" here does not necessarily mean something negative. For example, locating the hotel that we already have booked is a problem. Deciding where we will go to eat is a problem. We don't know what restaurant will have the best value, and so we have to examine a guidebook and menus to make that decision. Selecting the places of interest that would best use our time is a problem; Nancy and I needed to have conversation to evaluate what places of interest would best suit our schedule. What we enjoy about what places to see and what restaurants to visit is that the decision has been made by us and not by others. Whereas some people might find working through these problem areas to be tedious, Nancy and I find delight in these things. We like doing the research, making decisions, using our wits, and engaging local inhabitants with questions. When we start the process, we sometimes feel that we are being described by the words of the title of this book--"upside-down and blindfolded." The trick is to get ourselves righted and, at least in Nancy's case, to keep the blindfold off. Amazingly, we perform this feat again and again. As we did so and hopped along in our travels, we both felt an exuberance that added joy to our lives and has kept us taking trip after trip.

Printed in the United States
214500BV00001B/4/P

9 781440 128196